EMPOWERING
HISPANIC
LEADERS

AN ONLINE MODEL

Victor H. Cuartas, D.Min.

Library of Congress Cataloging-in-Publication Data

Victor H. Cuartas

EMPOWERING HISPANIC LEADERS: An Online Model

ISBN 978-0-9820875-5-8

DEDICATION

I heartily dedicate this book to:

- My lovely wife Isabel, whose love and support have blessed me so much in this process,

- Our miracle daughter "Eliannah," she truly is a precious gift from God.

- My beloved mother Maria Nubia, for her continuing prayer for me through the years,

- My brothers Diego and George for their encouragement and support,

- The Church of God family in the state of Virginia for their generous support and prayers,

- The Hispanic mentors, pastors, and leaders for whom I hope this project will be a tremendous blessing.

ACKNOWLEDGEMENTS

I am so thankful to the Lord for the strength and opportunity that He gave me to develop this book and the doctoral project on which it is based. The achievement of this project would not have been possible without the faithful support of my wife Isabel. She has fully supported my studies and ministry during the fifteen `years we have been married. I am so thankful for her obedience to the Lord that has allowed me to willingly respond to God's call in our ministry.

I thank my co laborers and friends in the ministry for their love and faithful support in prayer: José González, Rev. Juan D. Gonzáles, Rev. Miguel Dabul, Rev. Benito Fonseca, along with all the Hispanic pastors of the area. They inspired me to go deeper and trust in the Lord for developing this project to bless the Hispanic community.

I thank my Dissertation Committee for their advice and encouragement that helped me to finish this project: Dr. Wie L. Tjiong, Dr. Randall Pannell, and Dr. Miguel Álvarez. I am also thankful to the D. Min. cohort of 2003 from the School of Divinity for their love and friendship that blessed me throughout this process.

I thank the Center for Latin American Studies for their support and friendship during this project: Dr. Sergio Matviuk, Dr. Marcela Matviuk, and Dr. Rodrigo Zárate. They helped me to better understand the process, and it was a blessing for me to partner with them to develop this program. Dr. Marcela Matviuk also helped me to better analyze the results and statistics of this project.

I thank all the Hispanic pastors and emerging leaders who registered for the Hispanic Leadership Certificate Program at Regent University, especially my friends Pastor Wilmer Franco and his wife Claudia from Gainesville, Virginia. Their support and trust in this project was so evident and so vitally needed. The twenty-two students that participated in this program contributed something special and helped me accomplish this project for God's glory.

And finally, and certainly above all, I extend thanks to our heavenly Father for His faithfulness and love to me and my family throughout these years, to the powerful Holy Spirit for his guidance and wisdom to develop this project, and to our Lord and Savior Jesus Christ, who strengthens me and gave me the grace and favor to accomplish this program to expand God's kingdom.

CONTENTS

PREFACE

Dr. Victor H. Cuartas reminds us of the crucial nature of evangelism and church starting among the rapidly increasing Hispanic populations in the United States. He accurately and convincingly emphasizes the central place of leadership in any anticipated advance in church ministry among these significant groups. Dr. Cuartas points to the continuing requirements for leadership and for methods to train both career and part-time leaders for these ministries.

Many have pointed to the staggering need for Evangelicals to seek avenues to reach and minister to Hispanics. We have responded to these calls for action. In contrast to many of these studies, however, Dr. Cuartas progresses to a legitimate plan for providing exactly this imperative training. He has developed a reachable plan for training leaders for Hispanic ministries.

The plan Dr. Cuartas has developed was not concocted in a sheltered environment or some "hot house" situation that is divorced from the real world. This plan, rather, grew out of a carefully structured project of seeking a method of training Hispanic leaders. The project was actually his project report for his Doctor of Ministry Degree program and the work shows a careful and professional approach of such a study.

A part of the value of Dr. Cuartas' work resides in the fact that the facts and truths he surfaces are applicable not only to work among Hispanics but to other segments of the population in the United States as well. Persons working with any population segment can find both rationale and guidance to methodology in this book.

EMPOWERING HISPANIC LEADERS: An Online Model, is one of the most significant offerings in the field of leadership training. Get this book. Read and digest it. Put the principles into action. In a world of tremendous needs, Dr. Cuartas provides guidance in the development of training plans for leadership among many peoples.

Daniel R. Sánchez, Ph.D
Director of the Scarborough
Institute for Church Growth
Southwestern Baptist Theological Seminary
Fort Worth, Texas

LIST OF ILLUSTRATIONS

LIST OF TABLES

ABBREVIATIONS

ATS	Association of Theological Schools
Bb	Blackboard System
CEU	Continuing Education Unit
CLAL	Center for Latin American Leadership
EMPC	El Mundo Para Cristo, in Spanish (The World for Christ, in English)
HLCP	Hispanic Leadership Certificate Program
HSP	Hispanic Summer Program
HTI	Hispanic Theological Initiative
NSHLTE	National Survey of Hispanic/ Latino Theological Education

GLOSSARY

Continuing Education Unit

The Continuing Education Unit (CEU) is a nationally recognized method of quantifying the time spent in the classroom during professional development and training activities. Ten hours of instruction = 1.0 CEU. One hour of instruction = 0.1 CEU. The purpose of issuing CEUs is to provide a permanent record of training and continuing education for individuals who need to submit proof of their continuing education to state licensing boards, employers, etc.

Formal Education

The hierarchically structured, chronologically graded education system, running from primary school through the university and including, in addition to general academic studies, a variety of specialized programmers, and institutions for full-time technical and professional training.

Informal Education

The truly lifelong process whereby every individual acquires attitudes, values, skills and knowledge from daily experience and the educative influences and resources in his or her environment—from family and neighbors, from work and play, from the market place, the library, and the mass media.

Nonformal Education

Any organized educational activity outside the established formal system—whether operating separately or as an important feature of some broader activity—that is intended to serve identifiable learning clienteles and learning objectives.

INTRODUCTION

This process toward the accomplishment of this project has been a journey of faith. Everything started on March 2000 when I spoke with a dear friend of mine, Jose Gonzalez; he is the president of Semilla, a Latin American Christian Leadership Development Organization that seeks the reformation of society and the transformation of the culture through the word of God. I shared with him about the need for connecting with the community and the importance of training Hispanic pastors and leaders for ministry. He immediately responded very positively and encouraged me to move forward. That was the birth of "Tidewater for Christ" project.

I started to put together a project for Informal Education. I organized and oversaw fourteen all-day workshops in Virginia Beach and Washington D.C. to equip Hispanic church leaders from the Mid-Atlantic area. Each workshop involved three Ph.-level instructors, handouts, visual aids and evaluation. The topics were:

Description of the Hispanic Community of Tidewater

    i. *Strategies to Reach out the Latin Americans in Tidewater*

    ii. *Enriching the Devotional life of the Leader*

    iii. *Understanding the Voice of God in Current Events*

    iv. *Christian Education and the Church*

    v. *The Importance of Partnership and Spiritual Covering*

    vi. *The Fatigue and Stress in Ministry*

    vii. *Mobilization for the Harvest*

    viii. *Retaking the Spiritual Weapons of Prayer and Intercession*

    ix. *Holistic Stewardship in the life of the Leader*

    x. *Dealing with Depression*

    xi. *Walking in the Freedom of God*

    xii. *Biblical Principles of Government*

    xiii. *Understanding the Heart of God*

Then, I also worked with Regent University's Center for Latino Leadership in a professional leadership certificate to empower Hispanic pastors and leaders for ministry. That was a non-formal education program. You will find all the specifics about this process in the book.

Currently, I am exploring possibilities with the School of Divinity of developing certificates and bachelor degree program, which is Formal Education.

The author designed the "Hispanic Leadership Certificate Program" in response to a need to train and equip Hispanic pastors and emerging leaders and to assist them in becoming more effective in reaching the Hispanic community. The program found its central base in the example of Jesus' model of leadership. The materials in these courses were created to help the participants better understand and appreciate the American culture and Hispanic worldview.

The target audience for the field trial of the project was the Hispanic Pastors and leaders residing in the Commonwealth of Virginia, specifically the Gainesville and Tidewater region. Twenty-two students enrolled the program including four pastors and eighteen emerging leaders. The curriculum included a combination of online and residential instruction. Participants who successfully completed the program received continuing education credits through an accredited university.

The non-formal theological training pilot program consisted of two classes, which were taught sequentially over 8 weeks. This program was based on a practical model and included the following characteristics:

a) Theological training targeting leaders and pastors,

b) Community exposure,

c) Facilitating group interaction,

d) Opportunities for networking and partnership, and

e) Practical oriented rather than academically focused.

All participants successfully completed both classes, "Biblical Principles of Leadership" and "Purpose of Leadership." The assessment of the project was completed quantitatively using a pre- and post-online survey to measure the impact of the program regarding the students' behavior and understanding of the Jesus' model of leadership. Qualitative evaluation included interviews of two students selected at random upon completion of the courses. Although all students improved in their knowledge of biblical principles according to the Jesus' model, statistical results should be interpreted with caution since the sample size was small. The study also provides recommendations for future study and adaptations.

CHAPTER 1

THE NEED FOR TRAINING FOR HISPANIC LEADERS

This book offers suggestions for training Hispanic leaders who will serve the Lord in various regions of the United States. The author developed the materials in seeking the degree with Regent University, Virginia. The findings of this research project produced information, understanding, and direction that can contribute to the imperative efforts to train leaders for Hispanic groups everywhere. This book will, therefore, trace the development of the idea of the project and apply the findings to Hispanic training around the United States and other nations as well.

The material in chapter one provides the basic information that will help readers understand the reasons for the project that formed the background for this book. I will describe the context of Hispanic ministry in the Commonwealth of Virginia as well as the Hispanic enrollment in theological institutions. I will provide a clear statement of the problem, the rationale why I did the project, the limitations on the scope of the project, and a brief description the methodology. I will reveal the results and contributions and will end with a discussion of the plan for evaluating the project. Most important, I will suggest how the results of the project can provide guidelines for training Hispanic workers around the nation.

The author is convinced that the principles uncovered in this study of Hispanic leadership training will prove effective in training leaders for various other groups in the United States and other countries. Leadership is intensely important to Christian ministries among all peoples. The effort described and analyzed in this study will provide guidance for efforts to train leaders for Hispanic leaders as well as for other groups.

Personal Involvement
with the Problem

As part of the His plan to bringing me to Hampton Roads, Virginia, the Lord led me to plant *El Mundo Para Cristo* (World for Christ) church among the Spanish-speaking people under the umbrella of the Church of God denomination. Part of my passion was and is to see the transformation of the people's lives, not only spiritually, but also in terms of practical training and leadership. Since the Lord called me to the ministry in 1986, I have had a burden in my heart for training leaders for the ministry.

I was born in the city of Cali, Colombia. I moved from Colombia to the United States in December 1997. My focus has been primarily on the burgeoning Hispanic community in the Tidewater area. I also have had the privilege of leading the *"Tidewater Para Cristo"* (Tidewater for Christ) project that is an outreach to the Hispanic community of Semilla, another local Hispanic ministry based at Regent University. The president of Semilla, José González, has been one of the influential persons that God has used to bring inspiration into my life to pursue this ministry project.

The goal of this project was to organize and implement a pilot program, "Hispanic Leadership Certificate," to train and equip leaders for effective ministry. Part of the vision was to organize different programs in the Tidewater area as a platform where Hispanic leaders and pastors can be equipped and trained for ministry. The overall purpose was to partner and network with Regent University through the Center for Latin American Studies (CLAL) and other institutions to offer effective training for leaders, pastors, and missionaries.

It is important to consider some important characteristics of the Hispanic churches in Tidewater. Currently, about sixteen churches in Tidewater are affiliated with different denominations as follows: Independent, Church of God, Assemblies of God, Baptist, Pentecostal Holiness, and Charismatic churches (See appendix 1 for an explanation of the demographics of the Hispanic Churches in Tidewater area).

The Hispanic pastors and leaders of Tidewater are praying for at least fifty churches by the year 2014. That means that at least three-dozen new Spanish-speaking (including some bilingual) churches must be organized. Additionally, there are about six Hispanic churches in the Peninsula.

The sixteen Hispanic congregations gather less than 2,000 people in all. I estimate that twice that number of Hispanics attend non-Hispanic, evangelical congregations. These figures mean that at most, only five percent of the area's Hispanics are currently attending an evangelical church. In other words, only one church serves every 300 Hispanic people who need to know about Jesus. It is also important to consider the trends of the Hispanic population in the USA.

The current population report, released in March 2002 by the U.S. Census Bureau, reveals that in 2002, 37.4 million Latinos lived in the United States. This figure indicates that Hispanics make up 13.3 percent of the total population. Puerto Rico is not included in the current population survey. Among the Hispanic population, two-thirds (66.9 percent) were of Mexican origin, 14.3 percent were Central and South American, 8.6 percent were Puerto Rican, 3.7 percent were Cuban, and the remaining 6.5 percent were from other Hispanic origins.[1]

According to the U.S. Census Bureau,[2] between 1990 and 2000, the number of Hispanics in Virginia grew from 155,353 to 329,540. Hispanics now make up five percent of the Virginia population and represent all regions of Latin America. Some 22 percent of the Hispanics in Virginia are Mexicans, another 22 percent come from Central America, 16 percent from the Caribbean, and 12 percent from South America. In the greater Richmond area, the Hispanic population has grown by 227 percent in the last ten years. This represents a growth rate seven times that of the U.S. population in general.

The U.S. Census estimations made in July 2002 showed that there are 378,060 Hispanics in Virginia.[3] There are approximately 60,000 Hispanics in Tidewater. Demographic tendencies indicate that Hispanic population growth will continue in a similar fashion in

7

the near and distant future. The Hispanic population is expected to double as a result of these demographic trends. Churches and leaders of the Hispanic churches need to be prepared for the harvest over the next ten years in the Commonwealth of Virginia.

I have been working in different projects with Hispanic work in Virginia since 1999. These organized activities include: (1) setting up fifteen different, all-day training workshops for community leaders; (2) teaching at a local ministerial training institution; (3) organizing two community-wide gatherings involving hundreds of people; and (4) helping to establish and maintain a fellowship of Hispanic ministers in Tidewater area.

All these activities and the fact that I am currently serving as pastor of a Hispanic church in Tidewater, provides me a better understanding of the needs of the community and the needs of Hispanic work in the area. The Scripture that God gave me for the ministry is Isaiah 42:6-7:

> I am the Lord, *I have called* you in righteousness, I will also hold you by the hand and watch over you, and I will appoint you as a *covenant to the people*, as a *light to the nations*, to *open blind eyes*, to bring out prisoners from the dungeon, and those who dwell in darkness from the prison (emphasis, mine) NASB.

During the last four years, I organized and put together a ministry team with the purpose of teaching and imparting important principles. The purpose is to "build up" the body of believers in Tidewater. This ministry is, in part, the platform that God has used to lead me to this point.

Hispanic Enrollment in Theological Institutions

I assessed the enrollment of Hispanics in the following theological Institutions in Tidewater area: (1) Regent University,[4] (2) Tidewater Bible College, and (3) Bethel Bible Institute. The enrollment of Hispanics in these institutions was low. Table 1 summarizes the percentage of Hispanic enrollment.

Table 1

Summary: Enrollment of Hispanics, School of Divinity at Regent University

	US Citizen	Puerto Rico	Intern-ational	Total Students	Number of Hispanics	Hispanics
Spring '04	10	0	3	568	13	2.2
Fall '04	17	0	3	563	20	3.6
Spring '05	14	1	3	620	18	2.9
Summer '05	9	1	2	485	12	2.5
Average	12.5	0.5	2.8	559	15.8	2.8

Based on this table, the number of Hispanic students enrolled in the School of Divinity during the years 2004 and 2005 was thirteen and twenty respectively. The highest level of enrollment was 3.55 percent during the fall of 2004. During most of these years, the percentage of Hispanic students who were U.S. citizens showed a generally positive increase from 2.2 percent.

Part of the reason for this increase in U. S. citizens is the fact that the citizens of the U. S. have more access to student grants and scholarship funds. One of the major challenges for the theological institutions relates to the new government regulations that make it more difficult for international students to receive visas for continuing their educations. Based on the above findings, the enrollment of Hispanics in the School of Divinity at Regent University was low. However, Regent University is currently making efforts to initiate an undergraduate program in Spanish. The potential for attracting new Hispanic students is high.

Table 2 shows the enrollment of the Hispanics in Tidewater Bible College (TBC) and Bethel Bible Institute (BBI). In general, the enrollment of Hispanics in theology programs is small. One possible reason for the smaller enrollment is the fact that the institutions have not been sufficiently aggressive in targeting the Hispanic community.

In addition, there is a lack of leadership and ministerial programs available in the Spanish language. Most of the Hispanics who are enrolled in the programs must be bilingual. This fact underlines the imperative of providing more training opportunities in Spanish. The goal would be that no Hispanic would be prevented from obtaining the needed training simply because of a lack of facility in the English language.

Table 2

Summary: Enrollment of Hispanics in Theology Programs in Tidewater Area

Institution	Period	Total	Number of Hispanics	Percent of Hispanics
Tidewater Bible College[5]	Spring and Summer '04	63	1	1.9
Bethel Bible Institute[6]	Spring and Summer '04	130	2	9.2

Thus, the Hispanic Leadership Certificate Program offered by Regent University is important because it contributes meeting the need for theological training among Hispanics.

Statement of the Problem

The aim of this research was to initiate and develop a pilot project entitled "Hispanic Leadership Certificate Program" (HLCP) in the Tidewater area, Commonwealth of Virginia. This Leadership Certificate Program involved three denominations in the Commonwealth of Virginia. The HLCP can be replicated to bless the body of Christ.

The HLCP was a joint effort with Regent University through the Center for Latin American Center lead by Rev. Dr. Sergio Matviuk. The HLCP was a nonformal training program that focuses on meeting the needs of equipping emerging leaders and pastors. As a result, training efforts need to begin from the ground level and build upwards. According to the U.S. Census Bureau, "*more than two in five* Hispanics in the United States *aged 25 and older* have not graduated from high School" (emphasis mine).[7] The level of education among Hispanics is low and this is one of the reasons why there is a lack of influence by the Hispanics in different areas of society in the USA. The churches and ministries, therefore, need to encourage education and further training among the Hispanic community.

To initiate and develop the HLCP program, I had to answer the question: "What are the characteristics that the HLCP needs to have in order to meet the needs of the emerging leaders and ministries serving among the Hispanic community in Tidewater?" First, I identified the needs of the Hispanic community to design a model for theological training. Second, this in turn, allowed me to meet the needs of the emerging leaders.

I conducted a survey among the key Hispanic leaders and pastors in the area to secure their valuable input. One of the most important aspects of the survey was that their contributions helped me to find the needs of the emerging leaders and also gave me essential information to develop an adequate curriculum that will meet those needs. This project is the result of networking and partnering of several denominations and ministries. A copy of the survey in English is in appendix 3-A and Spanish in appendix 3-B.

The main focus of this ministry project was to initiate and implement the "HLCP" to provide a solution of the lack of training among Hispanics that will serve the emerging leaders of the 21st century among the Hispanic-American community. I believe that this project is important because it assisted in solving the problem of not having relevant theological training among the Hispanic Americans. This project provided an important alternative as a model for training emerging Christian leaders for the work of the ministry. The prayer is that others may take this model and use it to provide training among other groups in the United States.

Rationale for Doing the Ministry Project

This ministry project is important because it deals with one of the most significant needs among the Hispanic Christian leaders in

United States. The need for training emerging leaders with the right tools so that they can understand the American culture and the Hispanic worldview is imperative. The need in the United States is not the same as in serving the Hispanics in Latin-American countries. *Most People in my opinion are like this.*

Serving the Hispanics in Dallas, Texas, or reaching out to the Latinos in the suburban areas of the Tidewater area requires different approaches. Each of these groups of Hispanics lives in a different culture and thus demands a different approach to train them. The model for training this new generation of Christian leaders, therefore, needs to be relevant and contextualized.

This ministry project should be of interest to mission-oriented people, church planters in bilingual settings, and teachers and leaders interested in targeting the Hispanic-American population. Great potential exists for ministry in multi-ethnic settings.

I selected this project because there was, and will continue to be, a need for a nonformal theological training program to reach out the majority of the Hispanic leaders. In terms of academic and theological training, there are several seminaries and Bible colleges in the Commonwealth of Virginia that are meeting the needs of the people. To train people for ministry is complex and needs to be practical.

The general topic area for this project is theological education training for Hispanic pastors and leaders. This academic training also includes: bicultural training, equipping for ministry, Hispanic mobilization, and church planting among the.

There was, and will continue to be, a need to rectify the lack of formal theological training among the Hispanic Americans. This ethnic group has become the largest minority group in this country and there are not yet enough theological-training programs in Spanish so that leaders and pastors can be trained to reach out to the Hispanic community in Tidewater.

There was a lack of trained leaders and pastors among the Hispanic churches in the area who can effectively reach out to the people. At the regional level, the Hispanic pastors have been praying for three consecutive years for the raising-up of new leaders and ministers who are trained to serve and meet the needs of the Hispanic community. The Hispanic pastors and leaders of Tide water are currently praying for at least fifty churches by the year 2014. This means that new leaders and pastors need to be prepared for the ministry.

Currently, there are about fifteen churches affiliated with different denominations as follows: Independent, Church of God, Assemblies of God, Baptist, Pentecostal Holiness, and Charismatic churches. That means that at least three-dozen new Spanish-speaking (including some bilingual) churches must be organized. Only five percent of the area's Hispanics are currently attending an evangelical church. In other words, there is just one church for every 300 people that need to know about Jesus.

According to U.S. Census Bureau, more than one in eight people in the United States are of Hispanic origin.[8] So the potential of reaching out to Hispanics from different countries from Latin America is great. The emerging leaders are going to impact not only the churches but also the communities where they live. Who is going to pastor and plant the new churches in the area? What kind of theological training are the leaders going to require?

That was why it was urgent to offer adequate training for those who are being called to ministry. What will happen if they do not have access to formal theological training that is relevant? This project was about the harvest (Matt. 9:37-38) and God's kingdom and this project was a response to meet the need of lack of training.

This situation implies the implementation of a new model of leadership and the convergence of different generations that come together with the same purpose, that is, to be effective in terms of ministry. The solution proposed in this book would go a long distance toward meeting this obvious need among Hispanic leaders.

Method Used to Solve
the Problem

The model selected for use in the program was that of a non-formal theological training program. It was practically oriented rather than academically focused. The Hispanic Leadership Program promoted and facilitated useful training for Hispanic leaders, pastors, and missionaries who want to impact God's world through the Gospel of Jesus Christ (Eph. 4:11-12). This passage describes the individual offices of ministry and that implies that every leader involved in every office needs to have not only the anointing, but also the adequate training to function properly in that office. The target group was young-adults (20-35 years old) who have a heart for ministry and need to be trained to better serve the Lord.

It was the intention of this program to promote and utilize relevant resources and materials to equip emerging leaders to better serve their communities where God has called them. The HLCP was a joint effort with Regent University through the Center for Latin American Leadership.

The HLCP followed the cohort model so all the students registered for the program became part of the group and brought a sense of belonging and teamwork. This approach facilitated the process of spiritual growth because the students were working together by learning from each other during the whole process. The cohort for this program consisted of twenty-two students (four pastors and eighteen emerging leaders). The students registered for the program came from two regions of Virginia: Gainesville (fourteen) and Tidewater (eight).

The pilot program consisted of two courses (nonformal education). Each course lasted for four weeks. During the first week of the program, the students came to the Regent University Campus for orientation during which they received adequate instructions to begin the first course (On-Campus Session). During the following three weeks, the students participated and posted dialogues, including interactions with cohort members, by using Blackboard (Bb).

The students received a personal identification number and password to have access to the Bb. Before the beginning of the program, the students also received the necessary computer training to fulfill the assignments of every course. During the last week of each class, the students turned in a final paper in which they had the opportunity of applying key principles according to the instructions of the instructor.

The format of the on-campus session included the following alternatives for theological training: panel discussions, power point

14

presentations (audio-visuals), classroom discussion, small group interaction, case studies, guest speakers, etc. The all-day Saturday session included the following items: devotional time, praise and worship, teaching sessions (70 minutes length), discussion time and specific period for questions and answers, followed by closing in prayer.

This non-formal practical oriented model included the following characteristics: (1) theological training targeting leaders and pastors, (2) community exposure, (3) facilitating group interaction, (4) opportunities for networking and partnership, and (5) practical oriented rather than academically focused. The courses of the program are chosen according with the current needs that the leaders and pastors may have.

On the contrary, in the academic model (formal mode), the seminaries designed the classes based on the selected curriculum. Therefore, the student strictly follows the curriculum. In contrast, in the nonformal model the leaders and pastors have the opportunity to learn important principles related to specific topics that they have requested in advance.

During the sessions, the leaders and pastors who participated in the field trial had the opportunity to interact in groups and contextualize the biblical principles according to their specific scenarios. The purpose was to allow the students learn not only by the impartation of the speakers but also by the interaction with their colleagues. Every leader and pastor has access to this kind of theological training, and every local church will benefit from this practical model of training. This practical oriented model may vary according to the needs of the people.

This project was a paradigm shift in terms of new models of theological training. In addition, there was not distinction between laity and clergy training. By having adequate theological training, the emerging leaders and pastors are equipped, and through the ministry of the Holy Spirit, they fulfilled their call in the ministry.

The primary beneficiaries of this ministry project were the emerging leaders and the pastors who work and serve among the Hispanic Americans in USA. This project also will benefit the Hispanic believers that are bilingual and are actively involved in other churches--Anglo, Philippine, Asian, etc. These groups are important and need to be trained cross-culturally to be effective in their calls as bridges between two worlds: the Latino and the Anglo.I developed and wrote this project to engage emerging leaders and pastors who have a call from the Lord to primarily serve the Hispanic Americans in the USA. My prayer is that the Lord will use this material to greatly expand his Kingdom in the world.

Limitations and Scope
of the Problem

I designed this ministry project developed a model for nonformal theological training that will serve the Hispanic leaders of the area. This program has been initiated and developed to train emerging leaders among the Hispanic-American community. The Hispanic churches in Hampton Roads continued to lay down their own agendas in order to grasp a bigger vision for training leaders and pastors for the work of the ministry beyond the Tidewater area.

This project was intended to focus on the initiation and development of a theological training center that will serve the emerging leaders of the 21st century among the Hispanic-American community. This model was a nonformal theological training program. The main purpose was to offer additional alternatives for nonformal theological training of those who are called to serve the Lord in different capacities.

As a result of this program, the Hispanic pastors have a better understanding of the urgent need to prepare themselves for the ministry, and they are now more willing to send their best people to obtain theological training. There is a great need to reach out to those who are not yet saved. So far, I have organized thirteen Hispanic-workshops at Regent University. The response from the pastors and leaders has been good; this is the platform that God is using to show me in a deeper way the need for equipping and training the people for ministry.

I have been working in several projects and also having the opportunity of preaching and visiting almost every Hispanic church in the area. Thus, I have come to the conclusion that the most important need among the Hispanic community is that of training and equipping the leaders for ministry. *Probably all communities*

There is a desire for serving the Lord, but most of the leaders who are serving in the Hispanic churches do not have theological training. Therefore, they do not know how to minister to the people. I believed that one of the reasons for the lack of training in the churches is that many pastors do not know the options available even for themselves. Less than 30% of the pastors of the area have received theological training (academic or nonformal). This is critical and there is a need to bring awareness in our local communities of the importance to be equipped in order to have an effective ministry.

In today's society the people are looking for examples of leaders that they want to follow and not just for hearing good sermons in the churches. If Christian institutions do not offer theological training to equip the leaders for ministry, there is a risk of losing the harvest that is coming as a result of the outpouring of the Holy Spirit.

One major limitation of this project was the lack of computer competency among the Hispanic leaders and pastors as well as the lack of proficiency of English language. Even though the program was conducted in Spanish, it was necessary for the students to have some level of reading in the English language because of the use of the Blackboard on the Internet. The students received basic training in computers prior the initiation of the program; yet some of them showed a lot of deficiencies in this area. My hope was to continue partnering with other institutions to offer basic training in these areas (computer and language skills) to the Hispanic community. This will benefit them so that they have other possibilities for training.

Another limitation of the project had to do with the number of students registered for the program. I was expecting to have at least thirty students registered for the program, but that did not happen. Several pastors I expected to send leaders for the training backed out for legitimate reasons. A total of twenty-two students were registered for the program.

Due to the low number of students registered and some mistakes in the questions that I formulated in the student profile (pre and post), I was not able to evaluate the statistical results adequately. Instead, I evaluated the results of the program qualitatively.

Finally, the selection process for participation in the program needs to be improved. I allowed some students to participate in the program that later on I realized that were not ready for the program. I learned from this experience that it is important to establish the minimum requirements for the students to qualify for the program.

Brief Summary of Results and Contributions

I developed and implemented the HLCP in the Tidewater area. The four pastors and the eighteen emerging Christian leaders were blessed in their ministries. Te theological training center was the response to one of the most important needs in the area among the Hispanic population: the need for nonformal theological training.

One of the most exciting results from this program was that all the twenty-two students who registered were able to finish well. The project experienced no dropouts. This is important because according to the Census Bureau, the 1997 Hispanic high school dropout rate was the highest (30.6 percent) in comparison with blacks (16.7 percent) and whites (12.4 percent). The fact that the participants completed the project, therefore, was an important reality in regard to educational attainment. We believe that such efforts among Hispanics in the USA will provide similar results in the area of completion rates.

The students enrolled in the program were able to improve their computer skills. At the beginning of the program, five students (22.7 percent) did not have any computer skills (Internet access, sending emails, sending attachments, etc.). At the end of the program, all the students showed improvement in their computer competency as well in posting the dialogues through the Blackboard system.

The remainder of this book provides the details for the project.

Chapter two presents a survey of available literature that relates to theological training. Chapter three gives the biblical foundation for theological training and it presents Christ as a model of an effective biblical leader who trained others effectively. Chapter four details a description of the project. Finally, Chapter five summarizes the results, implications, contributions, and recommendations associated to some future projects related to training and equipping Hispanic pastors and leaders.

Summary of Chapter One

The aim of this project intended to organize and implement a pilot program entitled "Hispanic Leadership Certificate" to train and equip Christian leaders for effective ministry. The general topic was the theological education for training Hispanic pastors and leaders. The model used in this project was a nonformal theological training program.

The cohort for this program consisted of four pastors and eighteen emerging leaders. I designed this ministry project to develop a model for nonformal theological training to serve the Hispanic leaders of the area. This project is important because it assisted in solving the problem of not having relevant theological training among the Hispanic Americans and provided an important alternative as a model for training emerging leaders for the work of the ministry. The project and its results give promise of aiding in the training of Hispanic leaders in regions outside Virginia.

The methodology the author used for this project has meaning for ministries in various sections of the United States and among various population segments.

CHAPTER 2

TEACHINGS RELATED TO THE FIELD OF TRAINING

The writer divided the survey of literature into two basic categories. The first includes general works related to the overview of theological training, curriculum design, delivering theological education, leadership, and ministry. The other category deals with works related more specifically to Jesus' model of leadership, multicultural ministry, Hispanic American theology, Hispanic Ministry in North America, and the background and attitude of Hispanics toward theological education.

General Works Related to Theological Training

James Flynn, Wie L. Tjiong, and Russell W. West emphasize in their book, *Well Furnished Heart*: *Restoring the Spirit's Place in the Leadership Classroom,* the importance of values transformation in theological training. Effective training demands that the trainers place special attention on values and paradigms. The workers must identify the old paradigms and the values and adopt new ones. The values are the foremost assumptions that we believe are true.[9]

Aubrey Malphurs, in his book *Values-Driven Leadership*, discusses the importance of change based on values rather than mere structure. He affirms that values are the end that an institution is striving for. "The core values are the constant, passionate and biblical core beliefs that drive its ministry."[10]

Malphurs also mentions important elements for preserving the values through prevention such as recruiting, enfolding, enculturating, training, promoting, and rewarding.[11] He also mentions some ways to preserve values through correction such as challenging, enforcing and defending. I acquired key principles and elements that helped me review and redesign my core ministry values.

Flynn, Tjiong, and West also address important dimensions of theological education such as institution, process, faculty, and the dimension of the student.[12] I learned tremendously from this book, and it helped me to understand the process of theological education and the opportunity to implement some principles to train emerging leaders among the Hispanic community in the USA.

Flynn, Tjiong, and West have proposed a form of renewal-oriented training called the Convergence model that brings all of the renewal, contextual, and values-oriented issues to bear on the process of theological training. It is also important to allow the Holy Spirit to take control of the classrooms. It is important to evaluate the values that are at the heart of any endeavor so that teachers and mentors can choose the right methods to maximize the process in theological education.[13]

There is a current crisis in theological training. The different changes and transitions that have occurred throughout history in terms of theological training indicate the reality of paradigm shifting and values transformation taking place in the heart of the training process.

In *Reenvisioning Theological Education: Exploring a Missional Alternative to Current Models*, Robert Banks emphasizes the need for reenvisioning theological education.[14] I found Bank's approach helpful in regards to exploring a missional alternative to current models of theological education.

Banks deals with the urgency of developing a missional model, going from the margins to the center. There is a need for going beyond mission-oriented and developing a new trajectory in theological education. Banks defines the nature of learning in a missional model by emphasizing the closer connection between action and reflection and a more complete relationship between theory and practice.

General Works Related to Curriculum's Design

One of the most helpful books that clearly discusses the important aspects to design theological curriculum is Leroy Ford's, *A Curriculum Design Manual for Theological Education.*[15] This book offers an excellent description of the steps that needs to be considered to design a curriculum for Theological education. In chapter 1, Ford describes the meaning of curriculum and the implications in the real world. This chapter helped me to better understand the importance of establishing objectives and goals according to the curriculum. Ford also shares important elements about writing the course descriptions. This is one of the biggest challenges in theological training because there is a need for establishing the right goals and objectives for the theological programs. This aspect includes methods and learning activities, testing and evaluation approaches, and choosing the appropriate method for teaching.

Theological education needs to be contextualized according to the needs and background of the target group. The author implemented some of Ford's recommendations in the course of analyzing and describing the scope of the curriculum.

Lois B. Easton shares in her book, *The Other Side of Curriculum: Lessons from Learners,* important aspects and experiences from the point of view of the learners.[16] These lessons from the learners are vital in the process of designing curriculum for theological education because it helps me to consider certain things that I can ignore in the process. The best scenario for curriculum designers is to think as learners and teachers as well.

Easton also underlines two important approaches of the curriculum design: curriculum is learner centered, and curriculum is competency based.[17] Each of these is vital in the process of evaluating the results and success of the program.

Michael Connelly and D. Jean Clandinin their in their book, *Teachers as Curriculum Planners: Narratives of Experience*, treat he importance of teachers as curriculum planners using narratives of experience.[18] In section one of the book, the authors describe the parameters for understanding the curriculum. One of the points that caught my attention was the fact that the curriculum needs to be designed according to the specific target group. The authors state "different things to different people."[19] Connelly and Clandinin recommend other books for further readings.

Among the comprehensive works that this author found helpful concerning designing curriculum is the book entitled *Establishing Ministry Training*, written by Robert W. Ferris.[20] Ferris presents excellent principles that can be used as a platform to develop curriculum for theological education. Even though Ferris focuses this book upon missions training, it contains helpful insights for effectively designing curriculum.

One of the recommendations that Ferris makes in his book is the importance of building consensus on training goals.[21] His point opened my eyes to an issue that might have been otherwise overlooked. The identification of training goals is paramount in the process of designing any curriculum for theological education. The outcome goals must be transformed into training goals.[22]

It is imperative to understand the point of view of secular scholars in regards to education and the current trends in methodology. One cannot ignore the developments in curriculum scholarship that advance the field in several important ways. By analyzing them, one can find the best ways to design curriculum for theological education.

General Works Related to Leadership

I rejoiced as I found my own ministry trajectory reflected in Robert Clinton's treatment. The book, *The Making of a Leader*, helped this reader to understand better what the Lord is doing in his own life in terms of leadership.[23]

Clinton shares in his book three challenges for effective leadership: (1) each leader personally must be what God wants him or her to be, (2) each leader must be involved in training other leaders, and (3) leaders must be in tune with God's purposes for them.[24] I need to be more intentional about developing other leaders.

General Works Related
to Ministry

Among the helpful books that tackle ministry issues, the book entitled *Confirming the Pastoral Call* by Joseph Umidi is an excellent guide to matching candidates for ministry and congregations. The book is divided in three parts. In the first part, Umidi deals with the timing for relationship renewal. It is important to choose the right person for a specific congregation and vice versa; it is necessary for church planters to understand their call reaching-out and targeting the right people in ministry.[25]

Umidi emphasizes the importance of prayer during those vulnerable transitions.[26] Statistical evidence points to the fact that there is a lack of effective prayer among ministers today. Prayer is the platform that God uses for successful ministry.

In the second part, Umidi points out different models and methods to match congregations and candidates.[27] One of the sections I enjoyed the most talks about integrity issues that build the character of the leader during their lifetime. Integrity is an essential element in ministry. Churches are looking for godly people who are willing to be transformed and changed by the power of the Holy Spirit. True integrity is revealed during trying times.

The last portion of Umidi's book talks about different models and methods for the candidate.[28] Umidi deals with the question of motives, which he graphically illustrates as "love or lust?" Every person involved in ministry should ask this question in order to make sure that his or her motivation for ministry is appropriate.

Another comprehensive book in terms of ministry is *Working the Angles: The Shape of Pastoral Integrity,* written by Eugene Peterson. He shares about three angles on which we need to focus in ministry: (1) praying, (2) reading scripture, and (3) giving spiritual direction.[29] It is so true that these elements must be part of every Christian's daily walk in the Lord. Otherwise one will end up being a professional in ministry working just for a paycheck.

Peterson's comments about today's curriculum that is so weak to prepare people for ministry seem real, reflecting the reality that is all around us. Many pastors are resigning and leaving the minis try today. Some of them are going back to the marketplace because the lack of training and spiritual formation.

Many people attend seminaries to find God's call without having any clue about their destiny in life. There is a constant war and it is necessary to counterattack with prayer and intercession. The devil wants to destroy the nations by keeping the people away from the biblical principles. Relativism and postmodernism are questioning truth; many people do not know any more what the difference between the truth and a lie.

Peterson also coauthored another book entitled *The Unnecessary Pastor,* in which he and Marva Dawn identify four elements in Paul's letter to the Romans that add to his vital influence in pastoral theology: (1) his submission to the scripture, (2) his embrace of mystery, (3) his use of language, and (4) his immersion in community.[30]

One of the aspects that caught this reader's attention was the fact that Paul always was thinking about people. He mentioned over forty names throughout his Epistles. This fact demonstrates his approach and interest for people. He was sensitive to the people's needs and yet he also was radical about his beliefs.

Works Related to Jesus' Model of Leadership

One of the comprehensive books that treats the importance of identifying Jesus' principles for leadership and how these principles impact the way of how Christian leaders minister to others is *In the Name of Jesus: Reflections on Christian Leadership,* written by Henri Nouwen. The author talks about the simplicity of life regarding the stages in ministry. It is true that Christian leaders face different challenges and the way that they respond to those challenges will impact our whole ministry and lives.[31]

Nouwen also shares about the paradigm shift of being led instead of leading.[32] Everyone must be accountable and be subject to mentorship, surrounded by people who can speak the truth to him.

25

Roger Heuser and Norman Shawchuck in their book, *Leading the Congregation: Caring for Yourself While Serving Others,* share about the leader's spirituality. The authors point out Jesus' example by presenting three elements of his spirituality: (1) He carried out His ministry within the context of covenant community; (2) Jesus established a rhythm of public ministry and private time, and (3) Jesus taught by example.[33] Reading this chapter was especially useful because balance in ministry is vital

Works Related to Multicultural Leadership

One of the books consulted that was helpful to understand the importance of multicultural ministry was *The Wolf Shall Dwell With the Lamb: A Spirituality for Leadership in a Multicultural Community* written by Eric Law. Law emphasizes the fact that God is so creative in terms of His creation.[34] Every culture is rich in its essence and when people come together in a multicultural setting it is important to be aware of the differences so that we can approach the people in a correct manner.

I believe that unity in the middle of the diversity is the key. There is a strong message in this book to understand and respect the differences from every culture. The concept of the powerful and the powerless is interesting. I like the approach of Law who suggests that we should be able to move and act according to the circumstances. This requires flexibility and sensitivity for success in a multicultural setting.

The multicultural community can be transformed through the wise use of media in order to have a positive impact on the people.[35] Law emphasizes the importance of the group media.[36] This kind of media is very effective because is two-way communication. Leaders placed by God in different communities need to be able to communicate effectively to clearly transmit the message of Christ.

Another book that deals with multicultural context is Ray Bakke's *A Theology as Big as the City.*[37] This book helps the reader better understand the importance of contextualizing the Gospel in the city. It is important to have an urban theology to understand the needs of the people. The realities in the cities are vivid, dealing with social and ethical problems that are affecting the masses.

The needs of the communities in the cities are greater than ever, and Jesus gave us his example by walking around the villages in order to meet the needs of the community. The challenges are greater and the urban population is crying out for help. God places people in specific cities and communities with a purpose which cannot be ignored.

George Simons, Carmen Vasquez, and Philip R. Harris' book, *Transcultural Leadership: Empowering the Diverse Workforce,*[38] features reflections on values and meanings in the different cultures. These authors deal with values of different cultures and the challenge that transcultural leadership implies. The authors show the American experience of diversity in a global context. This book provides a case study based on the North American experience to better understand transcultural leadership and its pros and cons.

Simons, Vasquez, and Harris emphasize the fact that productivity must come from the conjunction of culturally diverse women and men.[39] In terms of leadership, it is necessary to understand the diversity and be able to adapt important principles that are needed. In order to work with a multicultural team it is necessary to be flexible and respect the differences.

The context is important to implement changes and develop the strategies that will work in specific environments.[40] For example, I have been targeting and ministering the Hispanic culture here in the United States. Even though we speak the same language, "Spanish," every country in Latin America has specific characteristics and that brings diversity and different mindsets to the table. This is an important fact that needs to be considered to design a curriculum for leadership training.

In *Christian Leadership in a Multiethnic Society,* edited by James and Evelyn Whitehead, the contributors reflect on the need for theological reflection in ministry. I noticed the importance that theological reflection has in terms of making practical decisions in the ministry.[41]

James and Evelyn Whitehead present a model and a method for practicing and doing theological reflection in ministerial environment. The model presented by the authors point out three sources of information that are crucial to decision making in modern-day ministry: (1) the Christian tradition, (2) personal experience, and (3) cultural resources.[42]

One of the most practical books that clearly emphasizes the importance of reaching out to different communities is Manuel Ortiz's *One New People: Models for Developing a Multiethnic Church.*[43] Ortiz inspires the reader to go deeper in terms of knowing his neighborhood. He emphasizes the importance of demographics, anthropology, and contextualization. This is an ongoing process that helps to better understand the strategies to ministry the people in the communities.

Ortiz describes the biblical foundation for multiethnic church development and defines five steps that are necessary to establish the new humanity: (1) to write the biblical position of the church in regards to unity, (2) to develop a mission statement toward multi-ethnic community, (3) to develop a philosophy of ministry, (4) to involve multiethnic leaders in the process, and (5) to plan ahead how to resolve conflicts.[44] These suggestions obviously hold out much promise in meeting the needs for more widespread training for Hispanic leaders.

Works Related to Hispanic American Theology

One of the comprehensive books written from this specific perspective is Justo González's Mañana, *Christian Theology from a Hispanic Perspective.*[45] González's book is one of the major theological works from a Protestant perspective with a Hispanic perspective. His book offers theological reflections on the basis of the Hispanic reality in the United States.

The insights of González are helpful to understand important aspects that need to be considered to ministry among Hispanics in the USA. His experience of his minority status as Hispanic American allows him to bring to the table important elements to consider in studying Christian theology from a Hispanic perspective. González emphasizes the importance of the ministry of the Holy

Spirit. This aspect is paramount for ministering effectively in every culture. González also describes the Hispanic struggle within the twenty centuries of Christianity and interprets the different aspects and doctrines in light of the Hispanic perspective and reality.[46]

In *The Spirit, Pathos and Liberation*, edited by Samuel Solivan, I found important aspects that need to be considered to understand the foundations of Hispanic Pentecostal Theology. Solivan does an excellent job by studying and reviewing the Hispanic American roots and the need for developing a North American Hispanic Theology.[47]

The need for a specifically North American Hispanic Theology that can answer the theological questions continues to be a most imperative comody. The influence of liberation theology in this regard has been notorious. Solivan recommends certain categories for articulating the Christian faith from a Hispanic perspective: (1) a Biblically grounded faith, (2) the nature and task of Theology, (4) the mission of the church, and (4) the Hispanic-American socio-political reality. These elements are needed to articulate an adequate Hispanic theology that is relevant.

One of the most comprehensive books that tackles Hispanic American theology is *The Liberating Spirit: Toward an Hispanic American Pentecostal Social Ethic* which was written by Eldin Villafañe.[48] Villafañe's book is an excellent approach to a Hispanic American Pentecostal theology and social ethic. His contribution is outstanding and his book certainly is one of the most important sources for this dissertation. This book forces the reader to examine the worship and spirituality of Hispanic Pentecostals and also to consider the social implications in the community.[49]

Villafañe elaborates a synthesis of the cultural, social, and spiritual background of the Hispanics by recognizing the importance of Pentecostalism among the Hispanic Americans. God's purpose is to bring liberation to His people so that they can walk in freedom. The Gospel offers a redemptive plan for the human kind and Villafañe recognizes the need for that freedom among the Hispanic Americans.[50]

Eldin Villafañe, Bruce W. Jackson, Robert A. Evans, and Alice Frazer Evans also offer in their book entitled *Transforming the*

City: Reframing Education for Urban Ministry an excellent perspective of the need for reframing education for urban ministry.[51] This book helps the reader understand more fully the importance of comprehending the reality of the cities, its politics, its economic infrastructure, its cultures, and its demographic composition as part of the process of training leaders to transform the society where we live.

God loves the cities and calls us to find ways to offer theological education to the emerging leaders. Villafañe, Jackson, Evans, and Evans present six frames of reference to understand theological education in the cities: (1) contextualization, (2) constituency, (3) community, (4) curriculum, (5) collaboration, and (6) confession (spirituality).[52] The author into pairs of emerging frames has placed these frames. This is a very helpful model because it helps to clarify some ideas about the distinction between models and examples.

Reconstructing the Sacred Tower: Challenge and Promise of Latino/a Theological Education, written by Kenneth Davis and Edwin Hernandez, contains excellent insights that help to better understand the Hispanic theology.[53] The content and research is excellent and this is a continuation of the initial research that Justo L. González conducted in 1988.[54] Davis and Hernandez recognize the importance of the growth of the Hispanics not only in terms of demographics, but also in terms of their influence of the leadership of the nation.

The growing presence and impact of the Hispanics (Latinos) in the US is evident. In many cities of the country, Hispanics are already more than half of total population. Davis and Hernandez present an excellent update in regards of demographics, socio-economic, educative, and religious trends that are affecting U.S. Hispanics.[55]

The extensive data presented in Davis and Hernandez's book facilitates the process of understanding both the advantages and disadvantages of the current theological education system. Most Hispanics religious leaders experience great difficulty in gaining access to adequate theological education. Davis and Hernandez also examine the policies of enrollment of seminaries and schools of theology.[56]

Works Related to Hispanic Ministry in North America

Alex Montoya in his book entitled *Hispanic Ministry in North America* present an excellent perspective of the different challenges that are involved in doing ministry among the Hispanics in the US. After discussing the demographic trends of the Hispanic population, Montoya shares their implications for ministry.[57]

Montoya emphasizes the importance of raising up new leaders so that the churches can meet the current needs of the people. This is one of the most important needs among the Hispanics churches in the U.S; there is an "urgent" need for equipping and training the future and the emerging leaders. Lacking that, the Hispanic communities will suffer the consequences of lack of leadership.

Dr. Daniel R. Sánchez has produced one of the most recent books that clearly and accurately discusses the reality and challenges of the Hispanics in the United States in his *Hispanic Realities Impacting America.* This book is also available in Spanish as *Realidades Hispanas Que Impactan A America.* The book, that explores the amazing growth of the Hispanics, is based on studies that have been conducted by such prestigious and reliable organizations as the Brookings Institution, the Hispanic Center of the Pew Charitable Trust, the Harvard University Kennedy School of Government, the Urban Institute, the USC Annenburg School of Communication, the George Barna Research Center, the U.S. Department Bureau of the Census, and other books and documents.

The author identifies ten realities among the Hispanics in USA: 1) The growth of the Hispanic American population has exceeded even the boldest projections of demographic experts. 2) Hispanics have spread throughout the country faster than any previous immigrant group. 3) The First Generation (the immigrants) has become the largest segment of the Hispanic population in America today. 4) The use of the Spanish language has increased in the past two decades. 5) Second and third generation Hispanics have made significant strides in educational attainment, yet the first generation lags behind. 6) Hispanics are showing more receptivity

31

to the evangelical message than ever before in the history of this country. 7) Hispanics are typically very conservative regarding social values. 8) Second and third generation Hispanics have made significant strides financially yet typically newly arrived Hispanics have the most difficult time financially. 9) Hispanic Americans are the group with the largest number of children and young people. 10) Hispanics have much in common with one another yet there is significant diversity among them.

Sanchez continues with ten additional chapters giving practical and sound direction for ministries among the Hispanics of North America. This book, in both English and Spanish, is an indispensable source for those who engage in ministry among the Hispanics. *Hispanic Realities Impacting America* could well be an important addition to efforts to train leaders for Hispanic ministries.

Works Related to the Background and Attitude of Hispanics toward Theological Education

One of the most helpful articles that clearly discusses the reality and challenges of theological education among the Hispanics in the United States is "The Theological Education of U. S. Hispanics" written by Edwin Hernandez, Keneth G. Davis and Catherine Wilson. The authors used data from the National Survey of Hispanic/Latino Theological Education (NSHLTE) and recommend that accrediting agencies organize networks of seminaries and theological schools that are dedicated to increase the participation of their Hispanics students, faculty, and administrators. The authors also advocate that seminaries expand their pool of students by partnering with Bible institutes and their pool of faculty by organizing alliances and partnering with Latino/ professional and educational organizations such as the Hispanic Summer Program (HSP) and the Hispanic Theological Initiative (HTI).[58]

The number of Hispanic and Latino students and faculty in the Association of Theological Schools (ATS) remains limited although urgently needed. In 1996, the enrollment of Hispanic students in the M. Div. and professional masters' programs was 956, or 2.7%, of the total number of students enrolled in these programs. In the f all 2000, there were 1,322 Hispanic students enrolled in these same degree programs, or 3.3% of their total enrollment. While enrollment of Hispanic students is growing, both in terms of actual numbers and as a percentage of the total, it is neither representative of the percentage of Hispanic presence in the U.S. population, nor is it growing as fast as the Hispanic/ Latino population in the United States.

The reality is similar for Hispanic faculty participation in theological institutions. In 1996, there were sixty-nine Hispanic faculty members in ATS schools from a total of 2,883, or 2.3 percent of all faculties. By the year 2000, 91 Hispanic faculties from a total of 3,286, or 2.7 percent, were serving in these institutions.[59] Consequently, Hispanics remain the most underrepresented ethnic group in ATS schools, both in student enrollment and among faculty members.

These statistics convey the need for networking and partnering among churches and theological institutions as well as facilitating and creating new avenues to increase the enrollment and participation of both Hispanic students and faculty. According to Hernandez, "the challenge for seminaries in this new century is to be lighthouses, to act with goodwill, and to embrace responsively the promise of diversity."[60]

Theological institutions, therefore, need to be more intentional and strategic in recruiting Hispanic students and also facilitating and promoting diversity among their faculties. Hernandez also presented three suggestions to retain current Hispanic faculty and to attract new ones. First, theological schools should recruit Hispanic candidates for doctoral training by identifying individuals committed to scholarship. Second, schools need to support talented students to complete the dissertation and its defense. And third, schools should offer opportunities for young Hispanics to conduct and publish significant research.[61]

In addition, Hernandez writes the most important article that presented the reality of Hispanics in terms of theological education, *The National Survey of Hispanic Theological Education*.[62] In 1994, the Pew Charitable Trusts commissioned a study led by Hernandez to assemble a panel to advise him in regards to the National survey among Hispanics. Hernandez's survey is so far the largest national study of Latino religious leadership ever conducted, and the results of his work led to the development and establishment of a fellowship program, the Hispanic Theological Initiative (HTI). This program is currently based in Boston, Massachusetts and has assisted many Hispanic scholars by offering scholarships for talented Hispanic leaders who want to pursue masters' degrees and doctoral programs in theology.

The National Survey of Hispanic Theological Education provided new and important data for our understanding of U. S. Hispanic reality in regards to theological education and its implications. Over 16,000 bilingual surveys containing 302 items were sent out to Hispanic religious leaders that explored demographics, personal experience, educational struggles, and achievement of educational aspirations.[63] Almost 2,000 questionnaires were properly completed, and these responses represent the single largest database collected from Hispanic religious leaders to date. According to Hernandez, administrators and faculty interested in recruiting and retaining Hispanic students should pay attention to what their Hispanic students are experiencing, especially financial and cultural barriers to their success.[64]

In general, Hispanic leaders are extremely interested in attaining higher education although this interest varies somewhat by gender, age, denomination, and other variables. Hispanics seeking further education will be increased if the theological institutions adopt strategic policies to promote and facilitate enrollment and establish appropriate funds to offer more scholarships and grants for all minorities.[65]

In Manuel J. Mejido's article "U. S. Hispanic/Latinos and the Field of Graduate Theological Education," he presents the enrollment and preferences of Hispanics in theological institutions.[66] He shares three negative consequences of the Hispanic student enrollment shortage among theological institutions. First, the insufficiency of Latino faculty makes it more difficult for courses and curricula to have an authentic Hispanic orientation. Second, the lack of Hispanic faculty makes it extremely complicated for Latino students to have access to Latino advisors, mentors, or dissertation committee members. And third, there is a direct relationship between the lack of Hispanic faculty and the scarcity of Hispanic scholarship.[67] These suggestions convey the urgent need for promoting theological education among the Hispanics. The reality needs to change for the benefit of the Hispanic emerging leaders who will serve their communities.

Furthermore, Kenneth G. Davis, in his article "The Attraction and Retention of U. S. Hispanics to the Doctor of Ministry Program" discusses the reality of U.S. Hispanics regarding the enrollment in the D. Min. program.[68] As part of the National survey conducted to Hispanic religious leaders, 182 respondents--134 men and 46 women--expressed an interest in the D. Min. program. The tendencies of Hispanics toward higher education vary according to age, denomination, and background. The top three factors identified as most important for improving the quality of degree programs among Hispanics were the following: (1) faculty members who would become more knowledgeable about Hispanic worldview and culture; (2) more supportive services such as counseling; and (3) increased financial assistance. According to the findings, the most important factor for attracting and retaining U.S. Hispanics to graduate schools is making accredited programs affordable.[69]

In addition, Rosendo Urrabazo in his article, "Pastoral Education of Hispanic Adults," states that the challenges of lay ministry formation are: (1) economic expectations, (2) recruitment, (3) costs, and (4) teachers.[70] Two of these challenges presented are related to finances. Thus, theological institutions need to continue expanding their capabilities to facilitate the creation of adequate funding to offer scholarships to promote and attract talented Hispanic leaders and pastors to their programs.

Summary of Chapter Two

In this chapter, I surveyed the literature related to the topic into two basic categories. The first category involved general works related to the overview of theological training, curriculum design, leadership, and ministry. The other category reviewed literature related to Jesus' model of leadership, multicultural ministry, Hispanic American theology, and Hispanic Ministry in North America. The context of Hispanic American theology and Hispanic ministry in North America are highly significant for understanding the dynamics and characteristics of theological training among Hispanics.

CHAPTER 3

BIBLICAL AND THEOLOGICAL CONTEXT FOR TRAINING

This chapter briefly reviews the background principles for non-academic theological training that is contained in the Bible. Beginning with the Old Testament, examples of leadership transitions are discussed from Moses to Joshua and from Elijah to Elisha, continuing with the New Testament examples and teachings of Jesus, Barnabas, Paul, and Timothy. This section identifies some biblical principles that can be used as a model for theological training among the Hispanics in Tidewater.

Old Testament Perspective

The Israelites often encountered difficulties and troubles. On each threatening occasion, God, in His mercy, raised-up strategic leaders to rescue and to restore them. In the Old Testament, people like Noah, Abraham, and Moses were used to lead and to prepare His people. In addition, He also sent judges, kings, and prophets to Israel to reaffirm His covenant with them.

The Principles from Nehemiah

Most of these leaders had key people under their authority who were trained to do the work that was needed at that time. For instance, God used Nehemiah to restore the walls of Jerusalem and Nehemiah trained and delegated specific people to rebuild the city

(Neh 3:1-32). The city was divided into four sections: northern (Neh 3:1-7), western (Neh. 3:8-13), southern (Neh 3:14), and the eastern (Neh 3:15-32). Nehemiah planned the work, motivated his leaders, and organized the workers to accomplish the task.

Just as Nehemiah trained his people, the theological institutions need to focus on training people for the ministry. The account of Nehemiah's work provides an important and practical guide for leadership training among Hispanics and others.

Two Leadership Transitions in the Old Testament

The focus in this section is toward the transition of leadership that took place between Moses and Joshua. Next, the study will focus on the leadership transition between Elijah and Elisha. This transition helps the reader to understand important principles that need to be considered in terms of modeling and equipping the saints for the work of the ministry.

Leadership Transition From Moses to Joshua

Joshua had a difficult task to fulfill since he was serving one of the most important leaders in the Old Testament. Thus, the people had high expectations of Moses' successor. Robert Clinton, in *The Bible and Leadership Values,* points out four characteristics that helped to pave the way for this transition:

> Moses has publicly transitioned Joshua into leadership. Joshua needs a personal confirmation from God and received it (Jos 1:1 ff, note especially 1:3, 6, 8). Joshua needs spiritual authority in order to succeed Moses as a leader. God promises that to him (3:7) and does it (4:14). Joshua faces a new and challenging task in a different locale than was Moses desert leadership.[71]

This transitional process helped Joshua by minimizing the comparisons between his leadership and that of Moses. It is important to recognize the process that took place in the life of Joshua to become Moses' successor. He was trained to be a leader; it was not something that could be done quickly or taken lightly. God's servants need to be shaped and equipped, and certainly Joshua was no exception to the rule. Some of the factors that helped Joshua in the process of becoming a great leader are instructive for today's leaders.

Joshua became Moses' minister

Joshua was able to observe Moses' leadership and to learn from Moses. He was named "Hoshea", which means "salvation" (cf. Num 13:8); however, Moses called him "Jehoshua" or "Joshua" which means "Yahweh is salvation" (Num 13: 16). He was selected by Moses to be his "minister" (NKJV, NRSV). As Moses' assistant, Joshua was present on Mount Sinai when Moses received the two tables of the law (Exo 24:13ff.). "He was also guardian of the tent meeting when Moses met with Yahweh."[72]

Moses gave Joshua charge

Moses entrusted to Joshua' several ministry tasks that involved significant responsibility. First, Moses delegated to Joshua the responsibility of organizing and commanding a detachment of Israelites to repel an Amalekite attack in the Sinai wilderness in Raphidim (Exo 17:9). Second, Joshua spied on the land of Canaan (Num 13:16). With Caleb, Joshua submitted the minority report which urged the people to go in and take the land (Num 14:6-9). As a result of his faithfulness and obedience, he and Caleb were permitted to enter Canaan (Num 14:30). As an example, Exo 33:11 records Joshua in his temple duties as he remained faithful to the task assigned to him by Moses.

Moses recognized Joshua's potential as a leader. Furthermore, Clinton describes important characteristics that Moses observed in Joshua's leadership. These elements are "faith, faithfulness, and giftedness."[73] God was preparing Joshua to become Moses' successor because Joshua was faithful. Joshua and Caleb were able to encourage a younger generation and guide them to victory. All of Joshua and Caleb's generation died in the wilderness, yet a new emerging leadership was prepared to deal with the adversities of the land.

Joshua Learned to follow the Holy Spirit's Lead

Joshua had a teachable attitude, so he was able to grow not only in his leadership skills but also in his character. He learned significantly from Moses even while Moses went alone to the Mount of Sinai. He learned patience and kindness (Exo 24:13; 32:17; Num 11:28). The guidance of the Holy Spirit was essential to Joshua's ministry, to his growth as a leader, and to his preparation to become Moses' successor. God commanded Moses to lay hands on him (Num 27:18).

Joshua received divine affirmation

The Lord told Moses to call Joshua to meet Him in the tabernacle to "inaugurate" Joshua into ministry (Deut 31:14, NKJV). Other versions of this passage are: "I may commission him" (NIV, NASB), and "I may give him a charge" (KJV). Joshua was commissioned by Yahweh to become Moses' successor. Joshua's appointment was recognized in public (Jos 3:7; 4:14). The Israelites honored Joshua all his life just as they honored Moses. This affirmation in ministry is highly important. As such, God affirmed Joshua and other people who would lead with him.

God promised powerful things to Joshua

The Lord is faithful and always provides everything that His people need to fulfill their call. In the case of Joshua, the Lord gave the assurance that He would be with him as He was with Moses (Jos 1:5). The Lord also told Joshua "to be strong and courageous" (Jos 1:6a, NIV). Joshua was told to obey the law that was given by Moses (Jos 1:7a). The Lord exhorted Joshua to depend on His Word and to meditate on it day and night (1:8a).

For every ministry that serves the Lord to reach effectiveness and have a successful outcome, the leader of the ministry must keep and obey God's Word. This obedience is vital. Finally, in Jos 1:9, the Lord encouraged Joshua "do not be afraid" (NKJV), "Do not be terrified" (NIV), "do not tremble" (NASB). The Lord promised Joshua that His presence would go with him. In Jos 1:1-9, the phrase "be strong and of a good courage" appears two times (Jos 1:6a, 9a, NKJV), and the phrase "be thou strong and very courageous" appears once (Jos 7a, NKJV). The Lord's promises to Joshua emphasize the obstacles and difficulties in ministry. It is essential to depend on the Lord always and also to be equipped to fulfill God's call.

Joshua finished well

Joshua was one of the few leaders of the Old Testament who finished well. Clinton describes these four reasons for Joshua's ability to finish well:

- a personal vibrant relationship with God right up to the end,

- truth which was lived out in his life so that convictions and promises of God were seen to be real, contributions as a pioneer and writer,

- and a sense of destiny that was illustrated by conquering the land.[74]

Joshua was an obedient and committed leader. God used his life to minister to the younger generation and to settle the people in the Promised Land.

Joshua died when he was 110 years old (Jos 24:29) and was buried at Schechem (Jos 24:32). Joshua sought to move the nation ahead after his own leadership with the challenge to faithfully walk with God (Jos 24:14-15). His final two speeches illustrate the importance of walking by faith and holding on to God's promises (Jos 23, 24). This is found especially in Jos 23:14: "Behold, this day I am going the way of all the earth. And you know in all your hearts and in all your souls that not one thing has failed of all the good things *which the LORD your God spoke concerning you*. All have come to pass for you; *not one word of them has failed*" (NKJV, emphasis mine).

Leadership Transition from Elijah to Elisha

Elisha was a prophet in Israel during the ninth century B.C. He succeeded Elijah, and his ministry lasted for half a century. First mentioned in 1 Kgs 19:16, his name means "God his salvation." Elisha was the son of Shaphat who lived at Abel-meholah.

Elisha was called and anointed by Yahweh through Elijah (1 Kgs 19:16). Elijah found Elisha by divine direction--not in the temple, but in the field. He became the attendant and disciple of Elijah. On his way from Sinai to Damascus, Elijah found Elisha at his native place engaged in the labors of the field plowing with twelve yokes of oxen (1 Kgs 19:19a).

Elijah approached Elisha and threw a rough mantle over his shoulders, adopted him as a son at once, and invested him with the prophetical office (1 Kgs 19:19b). The Israelites were in need of a prophet since the nation was becoming more involved in Canaanite idolatry with the approbation of King Ahab and his wife, Jezebel (1 Kgs 19:1-2).

Commentator Matthew Henry writes, "His heart was touched by the Holy Spirit, and he was ready to leave all to attend Elijah."[75] The "throwing of the mantle" (1 Kgs 19:19 NKJV)--or "cast his mantle" (KJV)--was a prophetic sign that implied the delegation of authority for ministry. There was a sense of urgency in Elisha's call; he knew that something more important than working in the field was imminent.

The new prophet requested a little time to share his new call with his parents before his departure with Elijah. The answer from Elijah was compelling: "Go on back! *But consider what I have done to you*" (1 Kgs 19:20, NLT, emphasis mine). The NKJV reads, "Go back again, for what have I done to you?" Elijah's response helped Elisha to make up his mind right away. As recorded in 1 Kgs 19:21 he became Elijah's "servant" (NKJV), "attendant" (NIV), and "ministered to him" (NASB). He did not resist the call or avoid the consequences of not obeying God's call (Matt 8:21-22; Luke 9:61-62).

Elisha learned from Elijah. It is evident that the prophetic ministry of Elijah influenced Elisha. For some seven or eight years, he became the close assistant of Elijah until he was taken up into heaven by God (2 Kgs 2:11-12). Elisha witnessed the dramatic experience of Elijah's ascension to heaven. "The chariots and the horsemen symbolized strong protection as well as the forces of God's spiritual presence which were the true safety of Israel."[76]

Even though there is little or nothing about Elisha's life in the Scriptures, it is implied that Elisha and Elijah were working together in the ministry. For instance, Elijah took his servant Elisha on a farewell visit to the groups of prophets at Bethel (2 Kgs 2:1), Jericho (2 Kgs 2:4), and Gilgal by Jordan (1 Kgs 2:6). "Elijah wished to face the experience alone unless the command to stay here (v.2) was a test of Elisha's faithfulness which was answered by the threefold refusal of Elisha to leave his master."[77] Elisha remained a faithful servant until the end of Elijah's ministry (2 Kgs 2:2, 4, 6).

Elisha's constant presence with Elijah "ensures that a witness was present at both the ascension and the sign of succession."[78] This is an indication that Elisha appreciated his master, and throughout the years, he was equipped to fulfill God's vision. In 2 Ks 2: 7 it is written, "And *fifty men* of the sons of the prophets went and stood facing *them* at a distance, while the two of them stood by the Jordan" (NKJV, emphasis mine). "These fifty men served as further corroborating witnesses to the final disappearance of Elijah."[79] The fact that this group of prophets saw the miracle becomes important later for Elisha's credibility as Elijah's successor.[80]

> Elisha received a double portion from God:
> And so it was, when they had crossed over, that Elijah said to Elisha, 'Ask! What may I do for you, before I am taken away from you?' Elisha said, '*Please let a double portion of your spirit be upon me*.' So he said, 'You have asked a hard thing. Nevertheless, if you see me when I am taken from you, it shall be so for you; but if not, it shall not be *so*'" (2 Kgs 2:9, NKJV, emphasis mine).

After the miraculous parting of the waters of the Jordan's river, Elijah asked his servant, "What may I do for you?" (2 Kgs 2:9); the response from Elisha was amazing. He requested a double portion of Elijah's spirit. "The request for a *double portion* (v.9, 'double share,' RSV, NEB, JB) was not that he might excel his master but that he should receive the eldest son's share according to the law (Deut 21:17)."[81]

This Old Testament law requires that the firstborn son must receive a "double portion" of his father's estate while the other sons received only a single portion. Another commentator affirms that the phrase "double portion" indicates twice as much as any other heir, not double the amount Elijah had.[82] Elisha asked a difficult thing and the right of the succession is now dependent upon his witnessing the departure of his mentor. "Elisha asks for a double portion in the gift of prophecy which his master is bequeathing to the other prophets."[83] Since God endows the gift of prophecy, no mortal being has the power to bestow it. The expression "nevertheless" indicates that God has the last word; He is the one who grants the request. God granted the request and it took immediate effect when Elisha parted the Jordan's waters and crossed over (2 Kgs 2:14).

In contrast with the dramatic ministry of Elijah, the ministry of Elisha was quieter. Elisha began his fifty-year ministry among the regular people of Israel at the end of King Ahab's reign (around 853 B.C.). He also, however, addressed the royal court without having conflict with the religious leaders as Elijah had experienced. Elisha performed twice as many miracles as Elijah. The sons of the prophets witnessed Elisha's first miracle, the dividing of the Jordan River. They acknowledged that he was indeed Elijah's successor: "The spirit of Elijah rests on Elisha" (2 Kgs 2:15, NKJV). "The prophets accepted his empowerment and his preeminence among them."[84] Now, he became their teacher, and "the president of the ancient seminary for prophets."[85] The account in 2 Kgs 2:16 shows that they still needed a teacher: "Look now, there are fifty strong men with your servants" (NKJV). This is the beginning of Elisha's ministry after being trained and equipped by Elijah.

Elisha's ministry was powerful, and he was used by God to perform many miracles, including the following significant examples. First, Elisha healed the waters in Jericho (2 Kgs 2:20-21). "Elisha's act was one of showing God's mercy to a community in time of stress."[86]

Second, the young men of Bethel mocked Elisha. As a result, Elisha cursed them in the name of the Lord, and two bears mauled forty-two of the youth (2 Kgs 2:23-24). God gave Elisha all the authority as a prophet. "With the utterance of a curse 'in the name of the Lord, the focus on attention in this incident is the word of the prophet.'"[87]

Third, Elisha multiplied the widow's oil. "A man from the company of the prophets has died, leaving his widow destitute and on the verge of having to sell her sons into slavery to pay her debts.[88] God used Elisha and multiplied the oil so that the widow could pay her debt and live with her sons (2 Kgs 4: 3-7).

Fourth, Elisha raised the Shunammite's son. Despite all he had done, Elisha had not yet matched Elijah's greatest accomplishment since he had not been used by God to raise the dead. In this case, a prominent woman provides hospitality for the prophet; her son died and he is brought to an upper room and placed on the bed. "The prophet lies prostrate on the dead body, and the boy is miraculously brought to life again."[89] It is significant to notice that 2 Kgs 4:12 mentions Gehazi, a servant of Elisha just as Elisha had been the servant of Elijah. This is a multiplication process of leadership that is important for ministry.

In addition, God used Elisha to perform other important miracles. "The next two miracles of Elisha are grouped together at this point because they both deal with food." [90] For instance, Elisha purified the pot of stew. The writer of 2 Kings records first the moment when Elisha purified a poisonous pot of stew, and he also emphasizes the fact that Elisha fed one hundred men with twenty loaves of barley bread (2 Kgs 4:38-44). Elisha worked in a political arena with the alliance of three kings (2 Kgs 3:13-20), and he also ministered pastorally with needy people in domestic circumstances (2 Kgs 4:1-44).

Continuing in 2 Kings 5, Elisha ministered in another area, international politics; he deals with Naaman, an important Syrian general. "The narrative traces the miracle from leprosy to healing, accomplished by the prophet, so that it exhibits yet another example of the wonder of Elisha's power."[91] Naaman's flesh was restored and "became clean like that of a young boy" (2 Kgs 5:1-19a, NIV).

Finally, Elisha performed the miracle of the ax head. This miracle of Elisha's ministry, found in 2 Kings 6, is a miracle of provision for the needy disciples. Due to lack of space, the company of the prophets decided to build a larger home. During the building process, one of the prophets lost an iron ax head in the Jordan River; miraculously the prophet Elisha made the iron head float (2 Kgs 6:1-7).

Elisha's death was significant. The Scripture records, "Then *Elisha died*, and they *buried him*. And the raiding bands from Moab invaded the land in the spring of the year" (2 Kgs 13:20, NKJV, emphasis mine). In death, Elisha is claimed to possess the miraculous power Elijah had in life (2 Kgs 4:32-37; 1 Kgs 17:21-24). Elisha's death was not as remarkable as his master's. In contrast to Elijah's ascension, Elisha's burial was more common.[92]

Elisha continued his influence throughout the years: "So it was, as they were burying a man, that suddenly they spied a band of raiders; and they put the man in the tomb of Elisha; and when the man was let down and *touched the bones of Elisha*, he revived and stood on his feet" (2 Kgs 13:21, NKJV, emphasis mine). Not even death brings to an end this prophet's ministry; even an attempt of desecration results in a miracle. The deceased man revives. "Elisha has kept giving life after he has died."[93]

Lessons from Leadership Transitions

These are some lessons that we can learn from leadership transitions:

- God is always faithful with His people. He gives the leadership and direction that is needed for specific times.
- God provides all the necessary things that the chosen leader needs to fulfill His purpose.
- New leaders need to recognize and honor the ones who have been before them. They need to have a sense of destiny.
- The ministry of the Holy Spirit is paramount in leadership transitions.
- Leaders need to learn to keep and obey God's word.
- Leaders need to have a teachable attitude.
- Leaders are required to have a vibrant relationship with God to finish well.
- Leadership transitions are opportunities given by God to renew trusting and confidence.

- The success of leadership transitions depends on the willingness and boldness from the people to believe that God still is in control.
- Leadership transitions are never easy; however they are necessary to fulfill God's purposes in our lives.

New Testament Perspective

As was true in the Old Testament, the New Testament demonstrates a distinctive perspective on leadership and leadership transitions. The primary example of leadership in the New Testament comes from the life and teachings of Jesus. Readers can, however, find other examples of leadership principles in the lives of Barnabas and Paul.

The Leadership Example Of Jesus

Jesus' ministry represented the most important example to follow in terms of leadership. The model of leadership that Jesus implemented in the process of training His disciples is helpful for developing new training models for emerging leaders and pastors. Jesus' strategy for their preparation followed the biblical model that will be discussed in this section.

Jesus' Preparation for Ministry

Jesus Christ, our Savior, spent time in preparation to fulfill His Father's will on earth. He spent thirty years of His life mostly in solitude gaining insights from His father as He studied for the ministry. "He had gradually attained, in thirty years of education, in work, and in thought, a clear conception of His mission, of the career that lay before Him and its ultimate issue."[94] It is important to notice that the public ministry of Jesus was just three years in contrast with thirty years of preparation. That infers that "preparation" and "training" is important for ministry. Therefore, Jesus' example needs to be followed. If He spent specific time in preparation, how much more do others need to do?

In His preparation, Jesus relied on Scriptures and the Holy Spirit. In addition, William Blaikie affirms that the three sources

46

that Jesus used for His theological preparation were: (1) The Old Testament, (2) the book of nature, and (3) the human heart.[95] He mastered these sources well. His direct relationship with God and the Holy Spirit provided the powerful elements to fulfill God's will, "To conquer the earth for His father through salvation." Consequently, Jesus was divinely prepared for His mission among people. In Isa. 55:8 it is written, "For my thoughts *are* not your thoughts, neither *are* your ways my ways, saith the LORD" (KJV).

Jesus was fully man, and yet fully divine. One of the most remarkable things about Christ's ministry, as described in the Gospels, is that while people noticed the human aspect in every action and word, Christians are not permitted to overlook the Divine aspect. His work as Messiah was empowered by God, and He ministered to the people with supernatural power. This was God's plan to redeem His creation.

There are not a lot of details recorded of the early life of the Messiah between the period of His infancy and public ministry. There are some assumptions that indicate that Jesus spent a lot of time in preparation for His ministry. Three facts must be considered as part of the early recorded life of Jesus: (1) the incident and dialogue with the doctors in the temple, (2) Jesus' submission to His parents at Nazareth, and (3) His example of obedience when he presented Himself to be baptized by John.

According to Blaikie, these three facts shed an interesting light on the discipline of submission that our Lord came under and the variety and completeness of that discipline.[96] He practiced the principle of submission and believers are called to follow His example. In Heb 5:8-9, it states, "Though he were a Son, *yet learned he obedience* by the things which *he suffered*; And *being made perfect*, he became the author of eternal salvation unto all them that obey him" (KJV, emphasis mine). A process was in place in the life of Jesus; the process of learning obedience and "being made perfect" was part of Jesus' preparation for ministry.

Jesus grew throughout the difficulties and adversities that He experienced. Theological training is about practically applying biblical principles in ministry. That is the reason why training ought to be practically oriented. Jesus modeled that principle by allowing God to equip His life to fulfill His Father's will. He learned through the experiences and suffering. Sometimes believers think that the stress and challenges through theological training are going to be over when leaders and pastors begin to serve the Lord in ministry.

The reality is that ministry comes with daily challenges, yet God used all that to prepare every believer to serve and minister others in need.

Jesus' obedience was proven when Joseph and Mary found Him in the temple. His response emphasized the fact that His Father's will was more important to Him than to follow the rules of His parents. Nevertheless, Jesus submitted Himself to them. As recorded in Luke 2:49, "And he said unto them, *How is it that ye sought me? wist ye not that I must be about my Father's business"* (KJV, emphasis mine). There are two things in Jesus' response: (1) the intimacy with God, and (2) His faithful obedience to God by focusing on His Father's business.

As an example, one of the most significant accounts from the Gospels is the time Christ prepared Himself for the moment He would be tempted by Satan in the wilderness. Matthew recorded the event: "Then Jesus was led up by the Spirit *into the wilderness* to be tempted by the devil. And when He *had fasted forty days and forty nights*, afterward He was hungry" (Matt 4:1-2, NKJV, emphasize mine).

Jesus fasted for forty days to be prepared for the temptation from the devil. The temptation apparently suggests something negative; however, a divine purpose was behind this situation in the wilderness. Matthew affirms that the Holy Spirit led Him into the wilderness. God allowed Satan to tempt Jesus. Without God's authorization, the enemy never would have had the opportunity to do it. The fact that Jesus fasted and was hungry showed that He was not exempt from human suffering. The temptation in the desert was part of Jesus' preparation. As a result, His powerful ministry drastically impacted the universe by equipping the twelve.

The Training of the Twelve

When Jesus approached the disciples separately, they had one thing in common; all of them were busy working albeit in different fields. Jesus chose people who were living common lives. The initial strategy of Jesus' plan was to recruit twelve men who could bear witness to His life and continue His vision after He finished the ministry commissioned to Him by God. As such, John and Andrew were the first men to be invited by Jesus (John 1:35-40). In Matthew's account, the names of the twelve are listed:

First, Simon, who is called Peter, and Andrew his brother; James the *son* of Zebedee, and John his brother; Philip and Bartholomew; Thomas and Matthew the tax collector; James the *son* of Alphaeus, and Lebbaeus, whose surname was Thaddaeus; Simon the Canaanite, and Judas Iscariot, who also betrayed Him" (Matt 10:2-4, NKJV).

He chose twelve men who were not perfect at all.

The disciples were different in many ways. This group of disciples was diverse, not only in terms of personalities, but also in regard to their professions. They were not chosen according to their own capabilities. They were normal men who fulfilled Jesus' agenda; yet they did supernatural things by the power that Jesus delegated to them (Matt 10:1). In addition, the disciples were obedient and faithful with their Master and Jesus equipped them so that they could carry His vision on earth.

Jesus' Strategy to Equip His Disciples

Jesus called the disciples in order that he could equip them to transform the world through His message of salvation. "Jesus was calling people to forsake the normal obligations of family and work in order to follow Him and support His mission."[97] The strategic plan of Jesus to prepare His disciples involved his working closely with them. The disciples learned by example. Jesus' approach was personal and He spent a lot of time teaching them. Robert Coleman in his book, *The Master Plan of Evangelism*, describes eight principles that Jesus implements during His training of the twelve: selection (Lk 6:13), association (Matt. 28:20), consecration (Matt 11:29), impartation (John. 20:22), demonstration (John. 13:15), delegation (Matt 4:19), supervision (Mark. 8:17), and reproduction (John. 15:16).[98] Jesus was diligent and effective in His training, and He took the responsibility of preparing the ones who later would carry on His legacy and ministry seriously.

The preparation of the twelve was relevant, and Jesus spent most of His time sharing and teaching them. There are three elements that Jesus followed in his efforts to equip His disciples: (1) Christ, a perfect example for His disciples, lived what he preached. He lived as God would live among men; (2) His purpose was clear.

He intended to save the people for Himself and to build a faithful church that would never pass away. His heart is for the families of the earth. He did not make any distinctions among people; (3) He planned the strategy to win. Jesus' purpose was to redeem God's creation so that they could glorify His Father. Jesus lived, died, and rose again according to God's will. The whole plan of salvation was motivated by God's love for the universe.

How Jesus Equipped His Disciples

For three years, the disciples experienced the best practical training that has ever been provided. Their Master was a mentor and teacher and the teaching sessions took place on a daily basis. The balance between theory and practice was significant. Christ's strategy to prepare and equip His disciples includes the following aspects: praying, teaching the Scriptures, focusing on salvation, imparting spontaneously, training continuously, and searching for the core principles.

The Importance of Prayer

Jesus spent a lot of time in prayer, which He modeled to His disciples from the beginning of His ministry. In Luke 6:12-13, it is written, *"Now it came to pass in those days that He went out to the mountain to pray, and continued all night in prayer to God. And when it was day, He called His disciples to Himself; and from them He chose twelve whom He also named apostles"* (NKJV, emphasis mine). Jesus chose to be alone for specific times in prayer with His Father. He prayed for direction in choosing the twelve men who would join Him to fulfill God's vision for the universe. "Prayer is a necessity of spiritual life, and all who earnestly try to pray soon feel the need of teaching how to do it."[99]

Certainly, it was not unintentional that Jesus often let His disciples see Him talking with God. The Gospels call attention to Jesus' practice of prayer more that twenty times.[100] The Gospels' account emphasizes the fact that Jesus exercised an intensive prayer life. For instance, Jesus prayed before He went through important decisions and transitions in His ministry: (1) His baptism (Luke 3:21) on the Mount of Transfiguration (Luke 9:29), (2) The Last Supper (Matt 26:27) in Gethsemane (Luke 22:39-46), and (3) during His agony on the cross (Luke 23:46).

Jesus taught His disciples to pray by example and emphasized prayer's importance. He did not impose it on them; rather, He kept faithfully praying. As it is written in Luke, *"Now it came to pass, as He was praying in a certain place, when He ceased, that one of His disciples said to Him, "Lord, teach us to pray, as John also taught his disciples"* (Luke 11:1-2, NKJV, emphasis mine). The disciples asked Jesus to teach them how they should pray.

Throughout His ministry, Jesus continued to emphasize to His disciples the importance of a prayer life and constantly elaborated the implications of prayer. Jesus emphasized to them from the beginning to the end of His ministry how relevant prayer is to fulfill God's vision. In addition, Coleman affirms, "Unless they grasped the meaning of prayer, and learned how to practice it with consistency, not much would ever come from their lives."[101]

Teaching and Applying the Scriptures

Jesus' work as a teacher was powerful. He not only mastered the Scriptures but also lived the Word of His Father. "Jesus was a teacher whose teaching was the basis of His authority."[102] Immediately after the call of the first disciples, Mark says that Jesus *"entered* the synagogue and *taught"* (Mark 1:21b, NKJV, emphasis mine). Then, in Mark 1:22b, it states, *"because he taught them as one who had authority and not as the scribes"* (NASB, emphasis mine). Jesus was far more than a teacher; He was certainly a prophet of the Lord. "It is remarkable that even in the earlier days of His public ministry before He could have acquired the facilities that usually come from experience and practice, His ability as a teacher impressed all kinds of hearers."[103]

Jesus used the elements of nature to explain some Kingdom's principles to His disciples (e.g., the fields, crops, and animals). He included these elements in His parables to facilitate the understanding of the people. Jesus inspired the people through His insights. "The parables are one of the most distinctive features of the teaching of Jesus."[104] As an illustration, in the Gospel of Matthew, the following parables are expressed: the parable of the sower (Matt 13:18-23), the parable of the tares of the field (Matt 13:36-43), the parable of the lost sheep (Matt 18:10-14), and the parable of the ten virgins (Matt 25:1-13).

It is necessary to remember the shortness of the time that Jesus and the disciples were together (probably three years). It is amazing the way that Jesus prepared His disciples in such a short period of time. Jesus used every moment with His disciples to share important principles with them. "Their time of fellowship was meant to prepare them for their time of service."[105] The ministry of the Holy Spirit was paramount in this process of equipping the disciples to transform and change the world for the Gospel.

Focal Point on Salvation

Jesus resolved man's problem, "the heart." Throughout His teachings and impartation, Jesus never lost His focus of sharing the message of salvation: He came to rescue and save the lost (Luke 19:10). Therefore, His message was clear: Christ, "the promised Messiah" was the only way to know His Father (John 14:6). As such, Jesus modeled to His disciples how to win souls. "Practically everything that Jesus said and did had some relevance to their work of evangelism--either by explaining a spiritual truth or revealing to them how they should deal with men."[106]

Jesus was passionate for the lost, and His main motivation was love. For instance, Matthew states, "But when He saw the multitudes, *He was moved with compassion* for them, because they were *weary* and *scattered*, like sheep having no shepherd" (Matt 9:36, NKJV, emphasis mine). Jesus felt compassion for the lost and responded according to the needs of the people. He was always available for the needy, and He was interested in healing the hearts of the people.

The power of His message transformed the lives of His audience; therefore, Jesus' example needs to be followed in every effort to train people for the ministry. Theological training has to do with equipping normal people to do supernatural things through love and compassion by the power of the Holy Spirit. Ultimately, it is about "ministering to the people in need." There is still a need to emphasize the urgency of sharing the powerful message of Christ that transforms and restores the lives of the ones who are able to believe (John 6:47).

Jesus Spontaneously Imparted

Jesus' methods of imparting were effective. He ministered and imparted not only to His disciples but to all the people who were present during the time of His ministry. Jesus was so creative; one of the amazing facts in terms of His anointing is that He was able to meet the needs of the people according to God's will. His methods of teaching did not limit Jesus.

On the contrary, Jesus used different methods of teaching and ministry to meet the needs of the people. He taught and modeled Kingdom principles as He lived among them. He ministered to the needy as He walked in the villages, imparting what He learned from His Father. Jesus went to the people, and He accepted them as they were. "His method of ministry was to conceal the fact the He even had a method. He was His method."[107]

Jesus never lost His focus of the ministry. His approach was very humble and sincere; He spoke the truth regardless the circumstances. He was spontaneous, yet He followed the agenda of His Father. The disciples learned as they watched. Jesus lived and taught evangelism before them in spirit and in practice. They observed how He served the community, how He loved the sinners, how He was compassionate, and how He rescued the lost. In Matt 20:28 it is written, "just as the Son of Man *did not come* to be served, *but to serve*, and to give His life a ransom for many" (NKJV, emphasis mine).

In the early period of the disciple's training, "hearing and seeing" was the main occupation of the twelve. "Eye and ear witnessing of the facts of an unparalleled life was an indispensable preparation for future witness-bearing."[108] They were in the process of being equipped, and later, they were sent to minister to the communities with love and compassion (Matt 10:5-8).

Training Continuously in Progress

The disciples observed Jesus as they were together many times, and the training started as soon as Jesus began to talk and share with the people. In some cases, Jesus emphasized the meaning, and the disciples asked many questions to clarify some principles. For example, when Jesus shared the parable of the sower with the multitudes (Matt 13:1-19), "His disciples began questioning Him" (Luke 8:9; *cf.,* NASB). As a result, Jesus began to explain to them the meaning of the parable. According with Coleman, Jesus spent three times the amount of time explaining this story to the disciples than He did in giving the initial lesson to the crowd (Matt 13:10-23; Mark 4:10-25; Luke 8:9-18).[109]

On many occasions, the disciples were astonished by the explanations and teaching of their Master. As an illustration in Mark's account of the dialog between Jesus and the rich, young ruler, Jesus confronted him about his wrong motivations (Mark 10:17-23). This young ruler was more concerned for his wealth than God's Kingdom. Jesus always answered with divine wisdom; the apostles "were *astonished* at His words" (Mark 10:24, NKJV, emphasis mine). As part of His strategy for training the disciples, Jesus took advantage of every opportunity to teach them important Kingdom principles. He was not limited by the time or the circumstances and gave Himself to them so that they would be fully prepared to minister to others.

Searching for the Core Principles

Jesus taught strategic principles to His disciples strengthening their character and convictions. Jesus did not try to convince the disciples right away; rather, he waited until they had conviction in their hearts. He was more interested in transformation than simply dispensing information.

The disciples experienced Jesus' demonstrations of God's Word as He taught them. His goal was not just to explain some parables but to change them by the power of His words that became "the transforming message." Luke's account states that on one occasion a disagreement arose among the disciples "as to which of them would be *greatest*" (Luke 9:46, NKJV, emphasis mine). The Master's response surprised the apostles because He told them that they needed to be like children. Jesus told them, "For he who is least among you, this is the one who is great" (Luke 9:48b, NASB). As such, Jesus focused His teaching on sharing core principles to His disciples.

Jesus' Model of Leadership in Mark's Gospel

Mark's account follows the period of time in which Jesus trained

His disciples for the mission. There are some characteristics that we need to consider regarding the training of the twelve: (1) they responded to Jesus' call (Mark 3:13) and followed Him, leaving behind all that they were doing; (2) they were "appointed" (NKJV, NIV, and NASB) and "ordained" (KJV) by Jesus (Mark 3: 14a).

The purpose for them was to be with Jesus so that they could be sent to preach the Gospel. They would learn from their Master, and at the same time, Jesus would know them better. Jesus acknowledged the urgency for training His disciples (Mark 3:14b); and (3) they would receive the empowerment from Jesus to "*heal the sickness and to cast out demons*" (3:15, NKJV).

The Disciples Before Jesus Sent Them Forth

Jesus used parables to teach the people. According to Mark's account, some of the parables that Jesus taught were: the house divided (Mark 3:23-27), the unpardonable sin (Mark 3:28-29), the parable of the sower (Mark 4:3-9), the parable of the light under a basket (Mark 4:21-25), the growing seed (Mark 4:26-29), and the mustard seed (Mark 4:30-32).

It is important to notice that Jesus explained further to His disciples the parable of the sower (Mark 4:13-20). Jesus spent additional time explaining to them the meaning of the parable. He asked them "Do you not understand this parable?" (Mark 4:13a, NKJV). Then, Jesus proceeded to explain to them with details the whole parable. "*But when He was alone, those around Him with the twelve asked Him about the parable. And He said to them, 'To you it has been given to know the mystery of the kingdom of God; but to those who are outside, all things come in parables'*" (Mark 4:10-11, NKJV, emphasis mine).

Jesus used simple things to teach powerful principles. Mark 4:33-34 reads, "With many *similar parables* Jesus spoke the word *to them*, as much as they could *understand*. He did not say anything to them without using a parable. *But* when he was alone with *his own disciples*, he *explained everything*" (Mark 4:34, NIV, emphasis mine). In addition, the KJV reads, "[and] He *expounded* all things to his disciples" (Mark 4:34b, emphasis mine). The verb "expounded" in the Greek is, *epiluo* that means: (1) to unloose, untie; (2) to clear (a controversy), decide, settle; or (3) to explain what is obscure and hard to understand.

There is a contrast between the method of teaching that Jesus used with the people and the one that he used with His disciples. Jesus spoke to the people in parables, "as much as they could *understand.*" However, "he *explained everything*" to His beloved disciples (Mark 4:33-34, NIV, emphasis mine). Jesus personalized His teaching according to the ability of His hearers to understand.

According to Mark's account, Jesus spent additional time teaching His disciples. Jesus wanted to be alone with them so that they could understand everything that He taught to them. During that time, they asked questions to clarify important principles, and Jesus answered their questions with wisdom and authority. This fact implies that Jesus took His responsibility of equipping them for the ministry seriously. The task ahead was not easy for the disciples; therefore, Jesus fully prepared them to fulfill such a difficult task.

Jesus and Practical Training for His Disciples

After Jesus taught important principles using several parables, He exposed His disciples to the field and performed several miracles. He wanted to evaluate how much they had learned from Him. Therefore, Jesus and His disciples went to the sea in several boats, and a great windstorm arose while He was asleep in the stern. They woke Him looking for help and He rebuked the wind and the calm became great. Jesus responded, "Why are you so afraid? Do you still have no faith?" (Mark 4:35-41, NIV). Consequently, Jesus contrasts fear with faith and equates fear with no faith.

Jesus continued performing miracles. The next miracle that Jesus performed was the healing of a demon-possessed man from the country of the Gadarenes. On this occasion, the disciples observed Jesus' authority when He delivered the man from unclean spirits. The power and authority of Jesus amazed all the people in that region (Mark 5: 1-20). Also, He restored to life Jairus' daughter and also the woman who had a flow of blood for twelve years (Mark 5:21-43). This was a lesson about faith: "And He said to her, "Daughter, *your faith* has made you well; go in peace, and *be healed* of your affliction" (Mark 5:34, NASB, emphasis mine). The disciples not only observed Jesus performing miracles but also learned how to pray against the windstorms, as well as for the sick and needy.

Jesus was rejected in Nazareth, His own country. The disciples followed Him and learned many things from Jesus. He emphasized the importance of faith to perform God's miracles. However, in His own country, "He could do no mighty work there, except that He laid *His hands on a few sick people* and healed *them. And He marveled* because of *their unbelief.* Then He went about the villages in a circuit, teaching" (Mark 6:5-6, NKJV, emphasis mine). Jesus continued teaching and imparting the vision with His disciples before they were sent out by Him.

Jesus Called the Disciples to Fulfill His Father's Will

The verb "called" in the Greek is *proskaleomai,* which means (1) to call to, (2) to call to one's self, or (3) to bid to come to one's self.[110] The NKJV, KJV and NIV translate the word as "called." The NASB uses the word "summoned" (Mark 3:13; 6:7a). Jesus invited "those whom He desired" (Mark 3:13, RSV). The initiative lay not with the disciples but with the Master. "A call to preach always implies a call to prepare."[111] Thus, the disciples were called by Jesus for a specific purpose: "to preach the Gospel of Jesus Christ."

Jesus Appointed the Disciples

The Greek word for "appointed" is *poieo,* that means "to make ready, to prepare, to make someone into something."[112] The KJV uses the word "ordained," while the NKJV, NASB, and NIV use the verb "appointed" (Mark 3:14). Jesus selects the apostles from the larger group in order to train His intimate team. "They were twelve in number, corresponding to the twelve tribes of Israel, thus pointing to the fact that Jesus' mission was addressed to the whole nation and to Jews everywhere."[113] Jesus' mission involved the whole universe, and His heart was for the world (John 3:16).

The purpose of the selection of the disciples was that they might be with Him in order to learn from Him and then go out with power to extend His ministry. "After the death and resurrection of Jesus, the commitment and the ability of the twelve would be crucial to the continued spread of the good news. So it is important to understand what Jesus called the twelve to be and to do."[114] For that reason, He spent all the time that was necessary to equip them. Theological training needs to be designed according to the needs of the community to be relevant. Nonacademic theological training is an excellent alternative to equip leaders and pastors for the ministry.

Jesus Trained the Disciples to Preach the Gospel

The verb "preach" in the Greek is *kerusso* that means: (1) to be a herald, to officiate as a herald; or (2) to publish, proclaim openly: something which has been done.[115] "Through intimate fellowship with the Lord, the disciples would received a commission 'to preach' and an authority (*exousia*, power in the sense of delegated authority) to heal sicknesses, and to cast out devils." [116] Jesus sent out His disciples to proclaim God's kingdom (Mark 3:14b; 6:12b).

Jesus Sent the Apostles Forth To Do the Work

On this occasion, the verb "sent out" in Greek is *apostello* that means: (1) to order (one) to go to a place appointed; or (2) to send away, dismiss (Mark 3:14b; 12a). Jesus "began *to send* them out *two by two*, and gave them power over unclean spirits" (Mark 6:7b, NKJV, emphasis mine). Jesus' strategy to fulfill His mission was to send His disciples in pairs. "Jesus' training of the twelve had by now come to the point that He could send them out to spread His teaching."[117]

Jesus continued to work in the villages, but the influence of His disciples could reproduce His ministry. The fact that Mark 6:7a says that Jesus "began to send them forth" (KJV) means only that he had not done this before. "Jesus sent the Twelve Apostles on a brief missionary tour of Galilee, since He could not reach all the hundreds of towns and villages."[118] Jesus felt at that time that His disciples were prepared to go out to fulfill His mission.

Jesus Empowered the Disciples

It is written in Mark 6:7: "And He called the twelve to *Himself*, and began to send them out two *by* two, and gave them *power* over unclean spirits" (NKJV, emphasis mine). The disciples received the power from their Master. The NIV and NASB use the word "authority" instead of "power" found in the NKJV and KJV.

The verb "empowered" in Greek is *exousia,* which means: (1) the ability or strength with which one is endued, which he either possesses or exercises, or (2) the power of authority (influence) and of right (Mark 3:15a; 6:7b).[119] The disciples received the divine impartation from the Lord. Even though the disciples were trained for the mission, they still had to receive the power from their Master to be effective in their ministry.

Jesus gave specific instructions to His disciples before they were sent out to preach the Gospel. Some of the important principles that Jesus included in His recommendations to the disciples are the following: faith, dependence, and obedience. Jesus commanded them to take just a staff, a purse without money, sandals, and only one tunic (Mark 6:8-9). Mark 11-12 emphasizes the hospitality among them, and this was crucial for their ministry. Thus, commentator Clarke affirms, "Perhaps Jesus means to forbid moving to a wealthier house, and in any case they would not stay more than two or three days in one village."[120]

The Disciples After Jesus Sent Them Forth

The commission of Jesus to His disciples described in Mark 3:14-15 is fulfilled in Mark 6:12-13: "So they went out and preached that *people* should repent. And they cast out many demons, and anointed with oil many who were sick, and healed *them*" (NKJV, emphasis mine). At this point, the disciples went out and did exactly what Jesus told them to do. They preached the good news with boldness. "The mighty works and the preaching of repentance in view of the coming Kingdom repeat the activity of Jesus."[121] The verb "to heal" in the Greek is *therapeuo,* which means: (1) to serve, do service or (2) to heal, cure, restore to health.[122] The disciples practiced what they learned for their Master.

At the beginning, the disciples observed how Jesus healed the people. On other occasions, Jesus took them into the villages so that they could be exposed to the ministry (Mark 5:37-43). Here, the disciples are already by themselves "doing" ministry. They applied all the principles that they learned during the period of training with Jesus. Jesus gave them the authority to perform miracles by His name (Mark 3:15).

The Great Commission

No passage shows the training of Jesus mor
of the Great Commission. In the Gospel of Matthew, _
the most powerful expression of the commission that Jesus ɔ
his believers:

> And Jesus came and spoke to them, saying, *All
> authority has been given to Me* in heaven and on
> earth. *Go therefore and make disciples* of all the
> nations, *baptizing them* in the name of the Father and
> of the Son and of the Holy Spirit, *teaching them* to
> observe all things that I have commanded you; and lo,
> *I am with you always*, even to the *end of the age*.
> Amen. (Matt 28:19-20, NKJV, emphasis mine)

Matt 28:19-20 emphasizes the need for "teaching" the nations.
The verb "teach" appears twice in NKJV. The mandate is to teach
others to obey everything that Jesus told us to do. After that
commandment, Jesus promises to be with us always. In other
words, He gives us all that we may need to fulfill His vision. The
NIV writes "make disciples," and this has to do not only with sharing Jesus' message, but also implies a life style.

For Christians to teach or disciple another person, it is important to be prepared and be willing to share with others what is
learned from the Scriptures and the Holy Spirit. It is impossible to
share with others that which the believer do not have. This passage expresses the urgency for equipping and training both laity
and clergy so that the Great Commission might be accomplished.
There is no distinction between clergy and laity. Every person that
has been called by God needs to be prepared and equipped for the
work of the ministry.

The Leadership Example of Barnabas

Another example is found in the New Testament in terms of
training and modeling is the life of Barnabas, who mentored the
apostle Paul. Barnabas followed the instructions that Jesus delivered in the Upper Room. During that time, Jesus taught His disciples powerful principles to empower leaders for ministry.

bas Followed the Instructions Of Jesus in the er room.

John's account proclaims that during the upper room discourse Jesus presented the pattern for empowering leaders for ministry (John 13:3-5). Jesus washed the disciples' feet to give them an example. "Jesus' inward awareness of his power and office did not deter his ministry to the men he had chosen and was trying to prepare for the final catastrophe."[123] Even in the most difficult times, He was focused on serving His people. In this dramatic scene, "Jesus, servant of the Father, becomes the servant of humankind."[124]

Jesus also explains the purpose of empowering leaders for ministry (John 14:1-14). He explains to His disciples the importance of believing in Him. John 14:12 says: "Most assuredly, I say to you, he who *believes in Me,* the works that I do he will do also; and greater *works* than these he will do, because I go to My Father" (NKJV, emphasis mine).

Jesus was preparing His disciples to fulfill the mission of His Father on earth. "Jesus wanted to impress on the disciples that he was not disbanding them in anticipation of his departure; rather, He was expecting them to continue His work and do even greater things than he had accomplished."[125] Jesus delegated authority to His disciples so that they could continue expanding God's kingdom. The disciples would experience "the power of prayer in His name, through which He will continue to work in their midst."[126]

Later, Jesus also delegates the power to empowering leaders for ministry (John 16:5-15). The ministry of the Holy Spirit is paramount to fulfill God's mission. "He was laying a foundation for the work of the coming Spirit of truth"[127] (John 16: 13).

Earlier, Jesus promised the apostles that the Spirit would remind them of His teachings (John 14:26). At this moment, Jesus promised them that the Spirit would guide them into further truth, which they could not bear at that time. "They will also be enlightened about coming events."[128] Both promises were fulfilled in the apostolic writings of the New Testament. These writings confirm the revelation of Christ through His disciples by the amazing work of the Holy Spirit.

Barnabas Mentored Paul

Barnabas saw Paul's great potential and imparted powerful principles into his life. The name Barnabas means "son of consolation" (KJV), "son of encouragement," (NKJV, NIV, NASB), the surname of "Joses" (NKJV, KJV), or "Joseph" (NIV, NASB). Joseph was the Hebrew name used at home, in the synagogue, and among Jews generally. "The surname *Barnabas* was possibly to mark the beginning of his function of prophet or teacher--if we accept the traditional derivation of the name from bar-nebhuah, 'son of prophecy.'"[129]

Barnabas was a Levite (Acts 4:36). "He is mentioned 33 times in four different books in the New Testament: 28 times in Acts, once in Colossians and 1 Corinthians, and three times in Galatians."[130] His name appears first on the list of prophets and teachers of the church at Antioch (Acts 13:1). Luke refers to him as a "good man, full of the Holy Spirit and of faith" (Acts 11:24a, NKJV). He was born of Jewish parents of the tribe of Levi. He was originally from Cyprus, where he owned a piece of land that he sold (Acts 4:36, 37).

Barnabas wanted to serve God and was obedient. "He divested himself of all worldly entanglements so that he could be completely free to move about as the Spirit directed him."[131] He brought the money and gave it to the apostles to meet their needs for living and ministry. Barnabas was especially noted for his generosity, implying that such was not an obligation, and maybe even unusual.

When Paul returned to Jerusalem after his dramatic conversion, Barnabas introduced him to the apostles (Acts 9:27). This is the first occasion in which Barnabas supports Paul as a leader. "Barnabas was the one who believed in Paul enough to vouch for him."[132] He sponsored Paul to the Jerusalem Christian leaders and saw the potential in Paul. As a result, Barnabas convinced the disciples of Paul's conversion.

Barnabas was an encourager, and he had the ability to recognize the gifts in other leaders. Also, he was recognized among the Jewish community as having leadership potential. He was willing to recommend others in the ministry. "That Paul was accepted by the

Jewish Christian leaders is evidence of the growth that had occurred in Barnabas' life."[133] He was also very sensitive to the Holy Spirit.

Barnabas Experienced God's Grace

Barnabas was chosen by the leaders of the church in Jerusalem to investigate the Antioch manifestation of Christianity (Acts 11:22-23). He was "full of the Holy Spirit and of faith" (Acts 11:24, NKJV), and he saw the evidence of God's grace and work. As a result of his ministry, many people were saved. God used him to empower and release other leaders for the ministry. Consequently, Barnabas was instrumental in the multiplication movement from Antioch.

After he assessed the situation, Barnabas established a sound base of relationships at Antioch from which the leaders could correct problems with the Gentile Christianity. In addition, he brought in a strong leader who could change it and recommended Paul into this Christian group. This is one of the reasons why theological training is important; there is a need for multiplication in ministry so that the churches can release the right leaders into the right communities. Barnabas was sensitive to the Holy Spirit, and he responded in such a way that many people were transformed by the Gospel.

How Barnabas Equiped and Empowered Paul

Barnabas was intentional in terms of empowering Paul for the ministry. The following action words based on Acts 11:25-26 describe the things that Barnabas did to empower Paul in ministry: (1) he *went* to Tarsus, (2) he *looked* for Paul, (3) he *founded* Paul, (4) he *brought* Paul back, (5) they *assembled* with the church, and (6) they *taught*.

It is important to emphasize the fact that Antioch was the place where the disciples were called Christians for the first time. In Acts 11: 26b, it is written, "And the *disciples* were called *Christians first in Antioch*" (NKJV, emphasis mine). Barnabas and Paul worked together and taught God's principles to the people in Antioch (Acts 11:22, 26a). Barnabas influenced Paul in such a way that the

63

Gospel transformed the whole region. Barnabas unlocked the potential of Paul's ministry and also encouraged and modeled giving in the Antioch's church. He mentored Paul in this. Barnabas was indeed a generous leader, not only in terms of finances, but also in sharing his time and talents with others. Later, the Jewish Christian leaders as apostles to the Gentiles recognized Barnabas and Paul.

Barnabas Empowered John Mark

In addition to Paul, Barnabas also trained his cousin John Mark (Col 4:10). Barnabas and Paul came back from Jerusalem after they finished their ministry. As they were ministering in Jerusalem, "they also took with them John whose surname was Mark" (Acts 12:25b). This verse implies that John Mark was exposed to the ministry as he went to Jerusalem with them. The account of the training of John Mark underlines the necessity of theological training to equip emerging leaders for the ministry.

Barnabas saw the potential in this young emerging leader. However, Paul and Barnabas disagreed over taking John Mark back on the next missionary trip (Acts 15:36-39). Paul and Barnabas took separate routes and thus resolved the dispute. Paul took Silas as his companion and traveled through Syria and Cilicia while Barnabas took his cousin John Mark and visited Cyprus (Acts 15:36-41). However, in the end, Paul would appreciate John Mark's ministry.

Leadership Team in Antioch

Barnabas and Paul were now recognized in the church of Antioch as prophets and teachers (Acts 13:1). "The Antioch church was a place where the leadership gifts of the church were sharpened and deployed."[134] When the leaders are equipped and remain faithful in the work of the ministry, God promoted them. Paul and Barnabas were sent together as a ministry team. They followed the example of Jesus when He sent the disciples as recorded two-by-two (Lk. 10:1).

In Acts 13:2-3 it is written, "As they *ministered* to the Lord and fasted, the Holy Spirit said, 'Now *separate* to Me *Barnabas and Paul* for the work to which I have called them.' Then, having fasted and prayed, and laid hands on them, they sent *them* away" (NKJV, emphasis mine). Barnabas and Paul were sent to minister among the Gentiles. Both of them experienced God's power as promised by Jesus Christ (Matt 28:18-20).

The Leadership Example of Paul

The Apostle Paul continued the teaching and practice of excellent leadership training that had been pioneered by Jesus and Barnabas. The example of Paul is no less instructive than the examples of his predecessors. Paul teaches effectively about leadership training.

Paul Trained Timothy

Paul shared with Timothy what he learned from Barnabas. Paul was great as a leader, missionary, teacher, preacher, and author. The Lord used Timothy in the recruitment of others. Timothy was apparently one of Paul's converts on the first missionary trip. He may have been converted in Lystra (1 Tim 1:2; 2 Tm 3:11). Paul refers to him in 1 Tim 1:2 as *"my* own son in the faith" (KJV). His mother, Eunice, and his grandmother, Lois, are renowned for their piety (2 Tim. 1:5). The only thing that we know about his father is that he was a Greek (Acts 16:1); therefore, Timothy was half-Jewish. He was already at work in Lystra when Paul came back on the second missionary trip (Acts 16:2).

Paul's Strategy for Training

Paul was intentional in terms of modeling for others. Clinton's definition of modeling is, "the use of various life situations to impress upon followers godly behavioral responses, values, convictions, paradigms, and leadership lessons in order to impact their lives with these same items."[135]

Paul needed an assistant. Even more than that, he needed a partner in the ministry. He wanted to take Timothy with him. Therefore, Paul circumcised Timothy so that he could take him into the Jewish synagogues (Acts 16:3, 1 Thes 3:2). "To be circumcised would avoid a great deal of trouble and open for him many doors that otherwise would remain closed."[136]

Paul devoted himself unconditionally to the developing and training of his followers for Christ's sake. "Leaders are more efficient after receiving training for their particular work."[137] Paul's method of training includes the following aspects:

Paul Taught Jesus' Principles

Paul was a great teacher, and Timothy was familiar with Paul's teachings from the Scriptures (Acts 16, 17, 18, 19; 2 Tim 3:10; Rom 16:21; 1 Cor 4:17). Paul urged Timothy to "command certain men *not to teach false* doctrines any longer" (1 Tim. 1:3, NIV, emphasis mine). "The timid and emotional young man was to give orders, for such is the meaning of charge."[138]

The second method was that of personal example. Paul practiced what he taught by modeling his approach to training leaders (2 Tim 3:10-17). "Paul expressed active examples on his commitment in order to resolute action."[139] 2 Tim 3:10 states, "But you have carefully *followed* my doctrine, *manner of life*, purpose, faith, longsuffering, love, and perseverance" (NKJV, emphasis mine). In his letters and his actions, Paul shows himself courageous, strong, and enthusiastic but also persistent in the midst of difficulties. Furthermore, Paul's love for Timothy was great (1 Cor 4:17; Phil 2:22; 1 Tim 1:2, 18; 2 Tim 1:2-4).

Paul also exercised a life of prayer. He was a faithful intercessor. He constantly rejoiced in the Lord, and prayer was part of his daily walk with God. He prayed for the leaders and churches (1 Thes 5:17, Rom 12:12), and he encouraged leaders to fast and pray as well (1 Cor 7:5). Paul also shared prayer requests with his leaders about God-given opportunities for reaching out and for effective ministry among the people (Col 4:3, 4; 2; Thes 3:1).

Paul Trained Leaders by Correspondence

Paul was able to equip his leaders through his letters. He wrote personal letters to Timothy, Titus, and Philemon. He also wrote letters addressing specific communities: Romans, 1 and 2 Corinthians, Galatians, Ephesians, Philippians, Colossians, and 1 and 2 Thessalonians. In all the letters that Paul wrote, his passion and love for the Lord and also for the people in ministry is obvious. Sometimes he wrote with his own hand (2 Thes 3:17), and some times he dictated to a secretary; consequently, Tertius wrote the epistle to the Romans (Rom 16:22).

In the first letter that he sent to Timothy, Paul gave specific instructions to the young disciple so that he "may fight the good fight" (1 Tim 1:18-20, NIV, NASB) and to keep his faith and good conscience. Paul trained and taught Timothy through the personal letters in addition to side-by-side training as they ministered together in different places.

Timothy was exposed to ministry with Paul on several occasions as he accompanied the Apostle in different events. Part of his training sprang from his services as an emerging leader. Timothy participated in the *Macedonian* happenings (Acts 18:5, 19:22-41). He was part of the evangelization outreach at Thessalonica (1 Thes 3:2, 6). He worked in the word oriented efforts at Berea (Acts 17:10-15). He experienced the turbulent exits from both cities caused by the opposition. He observed the ministry with Priscilla and Aquila in Corinth (1 Cor 4:17; 16:10, 11). In addition to these important experiences, the developing young missionary received the remarkable teachings from Paul.

The apostle Paul writes in his letter to the Romans that every believer has different responsibilities in the church, but we are one in Christ. "For as we have many members *in one body*, but all the members *do not have the same function*, so we, being many, are *one body in Christ*, and individually members of one another" (Rom 12:4-5, NKJV, emphasis mine). Paul talks about "function" or "office" in the KJV, and this is related to exercising the gifts in the context of ministry.

For instance, believer receives training from others and then begins to function in the body according to his or her spiritual gifts imparted by God. Many believers in the churches, however, have not yet discovered their spiritual gifts. These Christians need to function in the church and the communities. Involvement in the Lord's services make up a vital part of God's call to every believer. Concurrently with the call, God imparts His gifts so that the believer can function properly in ministry.

In 1 Corinthians, the Apostle describes the spiritual gifts that God gives to believers. Some theologians called these gifts, "the gifts of the Spirit." Paul writes,

There are *diversities of gifts*, but the same Spirit.
There are differences of ministries, but the same Lord.
And there are diversities of activities, but it is the
same God who works all in all. But the *manifestation of
the Spirit is given to each one for the profit of all*" (1
Cor 12:4-7, NKJ, emphasis mine).

Every gift given by God needs to be used for His glory. In that
context, every believer is called to exercise the spiritual gifts that
he or she has received by grace. The spiritual gifts are not for
personal benefit but for the *common good* (1 Cor 4:12b, NIV, emphasis mine) or "for the profit of all" (1 Cor 4:12b, NKJV). There is
a close relationship between the task of equipping the believers for
the ministry (Eph 4:12) and the need for every believer to serve in
the body of Christ according to their gifts (1 Cor 12:4-7).

When every believer exercises his or her gifts, the Church flows
in total harmony through the power of the Holy Spirit. The responsibility for pastors and leaders is not only to help them discover
their gifts but also to encourage them to exercise those gifts to
"edify" and "build up" the body of Christ. This aspect needs to be
addressed to properly design the modeling to equip emerging
leaders for theological training in the twenty-first century.

Paul and the Purpose of Practical Training

God has given spiritual gifts to all believers for the edification
of the body. Paul writes in Ephesians, "And he gave some, *apostles*; and some, *prophets*; and some, *evangelists*; and some,
pastors and *teachers*" (Eph 4:11). Paul describes the five-fold
ministry gifts given by Christ to the body of believers. These are
Christ's gifts for the Church. Every office has specific characteristics, and the idea is to complete the body of Christ to bring unity,
and not necessarily conformity in the Church.

Jesus is the source for modeling the impartation of the spiritual
gifts for the church. Biblical commentator Donald Guthrie suggests
that the ascension of Christ has resulted in the bestowal of a mul-
tiplicity of gifts that find expression in different functions, all of
which are intended for the edification of the church.[140] In other
words, Eph 4:11 describes the individual offices of ministry. This
implies that every person involved in every office needs to have

not only the anointing but also the preparation to function appropriately in that office. Eph 4:11a states, "He Himself gave" (NIV) emphasizing that all these offices came from Jesus to benefit His body to build up the church. Furthermore, J. Vernon McGee affirms that the Lord Jesus is the One who has the authority and is the One who bestows the gifts.[141]

According to Paul, there are three important elements for edifying the body: "For the *perfecting* of the saints, for the *work* of the *ministry*, for the *edifying* of the body of Christ" (Eph 4:12, KJV, emphasis mine). In Eph 4:11, the purpose of the five ministries is mentioned by Paul and is the focus of this section in the process of training emerging leaders for the ministry.

Paul taught that the purpose of training was that of "Perfecting" The Saints." The Greek word used for Perfecting is *katarismos* that means "complete furnishing" or "equipping."[142] This word is found nowhere else in the Bible and denotes a process leading to consummation. It also means "*a fitting or preparing fully.*" This is the central verb of Eph 4:12 "for the equipping of the saints" (NKJV).

In this passage, "saints" refers to God's people with no distinction between the clergy and laity (NIV). Since there is no distinction between clergy and laity in the Scripture, any training program needs to consider this aspect when equipping emerging leaders for the ministry.

A second purpose for training was for the "work of the ministry." The Greek word used for ministry is *diakonia* (diakonia) that means "service," the functioning of those who work in the different offices (Eph 4:12).[143] This is the same word that is used to describe the "deacons" in the church, and it is necessary to understand the concept of "ministry" and "minister," to design an appropriate model for equipping emerging leaders.

A third purpose of training was "for edifying of the body of Christ." The Greek word *oikodomeo* (oikodomeo) means the act of "building up;"[144] it is related to edification. The present participle literally means "the (ones) building" and is used as a noun, "the builders" (Matt 21:42; Mark 12:10; Luke 20:17; Acts 4:11; 1 Pet 2:7). Thus, according to Eph 4: 11-12, it is clear that the "work of the ministry" is related to the "saints" (believers) who need to be fully equipped and perfected in ministry by the five-fold ministers of the Church. God has given specific gifts to every believer so that they can operate harmoniously in the body of Christ.

There is also a strong message of *unity* included in these verses. Paul talks about unity in the body of Christ. In Eph 4:13, "Till we all come in the unity of the faith, and of the *knowledge of the Son* of God, unto a *perfect man*, unto the measure of the stature of *the fullness of Christ*" (NKJV, emphasis mine). The goal is to be like Jesus where every believer is called to exercise the gifts according to the impartation of the Holy Spirit. This final divine purpose of unity of faith implies that both pastors and leaders need to recognize and respect each other's anointing and the spiritual gifts that God is pouring out to His body. Based on this Scripture, theological training must be oriented to equip emerging leaders, both clergy and laity for the service of the ministry.

In his second letter to Timothy, Paul provides an excellent example of the importance of equipping and mentoring young leaders for the work of the ministry. He encourages Timothy to diligently continue in his ministry because Paul knew the challenges and the difficulties he had faced in his own ministry. Thus, Paul writes,

> You therefore, my son, be strong in the grace that is in Christ Jesus. And the things that you *have heard from me* among many witnesses, commit these to *faithful men* who will be able to *teach others also*" (2 Tim 2:1-2, NKJV, emphasis mine).

Paul refers to Timothy as "his son," and this expression reflects upon the closeness of their relationship. Paul mentored Timothy for many years, and he was expecting Timothy to multiply himself in others. There is a lesson about leadership here, and the importance of training others for the work of the ministry. In 2 Tim 2:2, Paul exhorts Timothy to share the principles that he learned with faithful men so that they will teach others to serve according to their gifts. Furthermore, theological training promotes the "multiplication process" that is so crucial for the development of new leaders in the church.

Timothy Ministered to Other People

A further teaching related to Paul's training of Timothy concerns Timothy's continuing ministry to help and train others. Timothy was selected for the office of an evangelist (1 Tim 4:14) and traveled with Paul on his trip through Phrygia, Galatia, and Mysia to Troas, Philippi, and Berea (Acts 17:14). Next, Timothy accompanied Paul to Athens and was sent by him with Silas on a mission trip to Thessalonica (Acts 17:15; 1Thes 3:2). Then, we find them at Corinth (1 Thes 1:1; 2 Thes 1:1).

During the apostle's second imprisonment, Paul wrote to Timothy asking him to visit as soon as possible. He requested Timothy to bring specific things that Paul had left that he had left at Troas, his cloak and especially the parchments (2 Tim 4:13). Paul seemed to value the presence and ministry of Timothy.

Lessons from New Testament Perspectives

These are some lessons that we can learn from New Testament perspectives:

- Jesus is our model to follow in leadership. He truly was a servant leader.
- Jesus spent time in preparing Himself to fulfill God's will on earth.
- Jesus relied on Scriptures and the Holy Spirit.
- Adversity can become our best friend, if we are willing to grow and learn in the process.
- Empowering people for ministry is paramount. Churches and leaders need to become intentional about it.
- Prayer is relevant in the process of developing new leaders.
- Leaders need to be sensitive to the needs of the people. Jesus is our great example.
- ̄   ̄   empowering require a constant process.
                     of the Holy Spirit is essential in leadership,
                     e substituted for other aspects.

71

- Leaders need to teach strategic core principles and values to be effective.
- Every leader needs to pray for wise people around their lives. Mentorship and accountability are very imperative in every season.

Summary of Chapter Three

This chapter described the biblical foundation of theological training. In the Old Testament, the leadership transition from Moses to Joshua and then from Elijah to Elisha is found. The most important example of leadership training was found the life and ministry of Jesus and how He prepared His disciples for the work of the ministry.

From the New Testament accounts, the focus is on Barnabas's influence on Paul and the impact of his ministry as the most important writer of the New Testament. Paul trained Timothy in the same way. Later, Timothy was able to train others for the work of the ministry.

CHAPTER 4

DESCRIPTION OF THE TRAINING PROJECT

In this chapter, I will include a detailed description of the ministry project. But before doing so, I will first briefly describe the context of this project, which is the Hispanic Population in general, and the Hispanic Churches in the Commonwealth of Virginia in particular. I will also include some information about *El Mundo Para Cristo* Church of God, where I am currently serving as pastor. This consideration of the background setting of the project will clarify the need for nonformal theological training in the Commonwealth of Virginia and in many other regions.

The process involved in this project has also enabled me to recognize more readily and fully the reality and the needs among the Hispanic churches in the Commonwealth of Virginia. I will present the profile of some pastors and leaders in Virginia and their preferences for theological training. Understanding these profiles will emphasize the need for equipping Hispanic pastors and leaders for the ministry. Finally, I will explain the Hispanic Leadership Certificate program to equip leaders, pastors, and missionaries for the ministry.

The Hispanic Population in the USA

The U.S. Census defines Hispanics as people who originate from Spanish speaking countries or regions. Hispanics can, therefore, originate from many different races. According to the census

2000, the estimated population of Hispanics in the USA is 35.3 million. Hispanics comprised 12.5 percent of the nation's total population. (This does not include the 3.8 million Hispanic residents of Puerto Rico.)[145]

The percentage increase in the nation's Hispanic population between the 1990 and 2000 censuses was 58 percent. Numerically, this was 13.0 million. Hispanics accounted for 40 percent of the increase in the nation's total population during this period.[146]

The number of Hispanic or Latino families counted in Census 2000 was 7.4 million. Of these, 4.8 million, or 64 percent, had children under 18; 5 million, or 67 percent, consisted of married couples; and 3.3 million, or 45 percent, consisted of "traditional families," i.e., a married couple with their children younger than 18. [147]

According to Census 2000, 16.1 million, or slightly more than half, of the nation's 31.1 million foreign-born residents were born in Latin America.[148] The size of the foreign-born population from Latin America has grown rapidly since the 1990 census, when it totaled 8.4 million. Census 2000 numbers include both the group quarters and household population.

According to the March 2002 Current Population Survey, more than one-quarter of the foreign-born population from all nationalities were from Mexico. Mexico provided more Hispanics in the United States than any other country. Cuba, the Dominican Republic, and El Salvador also ranked among the 10 leading countries of foreign birth in the United States.[149] Knowing the country of origin of Hispanics in the United States allows workers to design ministry strategies in more effective ways. The numbers from Cuba and Puerto Rico also indicate significant numbers. These data is graphically shown in Figure 1.

Figure 1
Hispanics by Origin, 2002

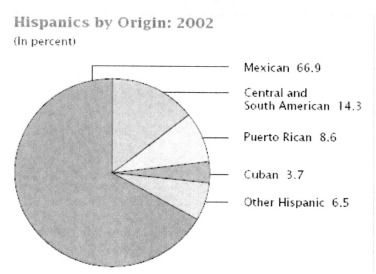

Hispanics by Origin: 2002
(In percent)

Mexican 66.9

Central and
South American 14.3

Puerto Rican 8.6

Cuban 3.7

Other Hispanic 6.5

Source: U.S. Census Bureau, Annual Demographic Supplement to the
March 2002 Current Population Survey.

The median age of the Hispanic population in 2000 was 25.8 years, meaning one-half were above it and one-half below this age.[150] Among Hispanic groups, median ages ranged from 24.3 years for those of Mexican origin to 40.1 years for people of Cuban descent. Approximately 34 percent of the Hispanic population is under eighteen years of age.[151]

The Ages of the Hispanic population impacts how the churches should approach this population. Those seeking to minister to Hispanics must obviously think in terms in those eighteen to sixty-four years of age. The large group fewer than eighteen must also win the attention of workers. Figure 2 pictures these facts concerning the ages of Hispanics and indicates the differences in Hispanic and non-Hispanic populations.

Figure 2
Hispanic Population by Origin
and Age Group 2002

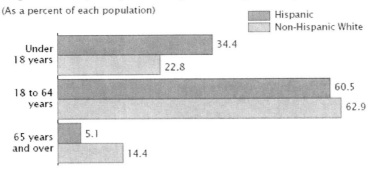

Population by Hispanic Origin and Age Group: 2002

(As a percent of each population)

■ Hispanic
▨ Non-Hispanic White

Under 18 years	Hispanic: 34.4 / Non-Hispanic White: 22.8
18 to 64 years	Hispanic: 60.5 / Non-Hispanic White: 62.9
65 years and over	Hispanic: 5.1 / Non-Hispanic White: 14.4

Source: U.S. Census Bureau, Annual Demographic Supplement to the March 2002
Current Population Survey.

In terms of jobs, 80 percent of Hispanic men age 16 and over were in the labor force in 2000.[152] Fifty-seven percent of Hispanic women were in the labor force. Forty-one percent of Hispanic workers were employed in service occupations or as operators and laborers in 2000. Fourteen percent of Hispanic workers were employed in managerial or professional occupations in 2000.

Hispanics are much more likely than non-Hispanic Whites to be unemployed.[153] The Hispanic workers earn less than non-Hispanic White workers. This discrepancy is due in most cases to the Hispanics' low level of education. The report of the HispanTelligence, however, showed that the unemployment rate for Hispanics dropped from 6.4 percent to 5.7 percent in March 2005, with Hispanics adding 214,000 jobs and 83,000 new Hispanics joining the U.S. labor force. Nevertheless, the unemployment among Hispanics remained 0.5 percent higher than total U.S. unemployment, which was 5.2 percent.

Also, the Census 2000 showed that the Hispanic homeownership rate—the percentage of Hispanic households owning their own home—was 46 percent.[154] This is up from 42 percent in 1990. Among Hispanic groups, Cubans and Spaniards had the highest ownership rates in 2000 (58 percent each).

77

Another important aspect is the Latino vote. While turnou Hispanic citizens in the 2000 presidential election—45 percent— was not statistically different from 1996, the number of Hispanic voters increased about 20 percent over the period.[155] This reflected growth in the number of Hispanics 18 years of age and older and in the number who were citizens.

In addition, a record number of Hispanics made their voices heard in Election 2004, with 7.6 million casting ballots. This infor- mation came from a preliminary analysis of a newly released Census Bureau study conducted by the National Association of Latino Elected and Appointed Officials.[156]

In regards to education, 57 percent of Hispanics 25 and over had at least a high school education in 2000. Only 11 percent of the Hispanic population 25 and over had at least a bachelor's de- gree in 2000. Finally, only 573,000 Hispanics 15 and over had an advanced degree (e.g., masters, doctorate, medical, or law) in 2000.[157]

According to Census statistics of 2002, the Hispanics showed lower rates of education attainment (high school and bachelor's degrees) in comparison with non-Hispanic Whites.[158] This was opposite in terms of 9th-12th grade, where Hispanics showed higher rates of education attainment than the Whites. The educa- tional realities of Hispanics in the United States is a critical consid- eration of those seeking to minister to the Hispanic populations in the United States. This is shown in Figure 3.

Figure 3
Population by Hispanic Origin and
Educational Attainment: 2002

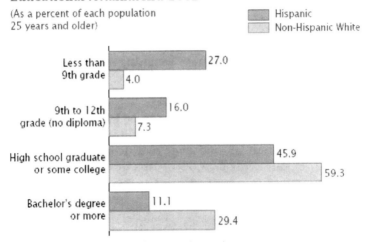

ation by Hispanic Origin and
Educational Attainment: 2002

(As a percent of each population
25 years and older)

Hispanic
Non-Hispanic White

Less than 9th grade — 27.0 / 4.0

9th to 12th grade (no diploma) — 16.0 / 7.3

High school graduate or some college — 45.9 / 59.3

Bachelor's degree or more — 11.1 / 29.4

Source: U.S. Census Bureau, Annual Demographic Supplement to
the March 2002 Current Population Survey.

The reality in terms of education attainment among the Hispanic community arouses concern. More than two in five Hispanics aged 25 and older have not graduated from high school. According to the Census Bureau, the 1997 Hispanic high school dropout rate of 30.6 percent is significantly higher than the 16.7 percent for Blacks and 12.4 percent for Whites.[159] This is shown in Figure 4.

Seeking to make great neighbors, great community advocates and organizers!

Figure 4
Population with at Least a
High School Education by Detailed
Hispanic Origin: 2002

Population With at Least a High School Education
by Detailed Hispanic Origin: 2002

(As percent of each population 25 years and older)

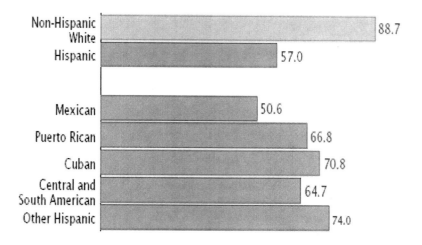

Non-Hispanic White: 88.7
Hispanic: 57.0

Mexican: 50.6
Puerto Rican: 66.8
Cuban: 70.8
Central and South American: 64.7
Other Hispanic: 74.0

Source: U.S. Census Bureau, Annual Demographic Supplement to
the March 2002 Current Population Survey.

Another factor that needs to be considered among the Hispanic community is the level of poverty.[160] Hispanics are more likely than non-Hispanic Whites to live in poverty. In 2002, 21.4 percent of Hispanics were living in poverty, compared with 7.8 percent of non-Hispanic Whites. Any progress for the Hispanic populations in the United States must take the poverty factor into consideration and seek ways to alleviate this problem.

Figure 5
People Living Below Poverty Level
by Detailed Hispanic Origin: 2001

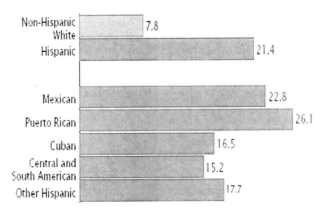

People Living Below the Poverty Level
by Detailed Hispanic Origin: 2001

(In percent)

Source: U.S. Census Bureau, Annual Demographic Supplement to
the March 2002 Current Population Survey.

Hispanics are significantly under-represented in the accredited theological schools in the USA. This reality affects the life of the Hispanic community since the moral and spiritual wholeness of the community is directly associated to the general well being of the community.

The Hispanic Population in Virginia

According to the U.S. Census, between 1990 and 2000, the number of Hispanics in Virginia grew from 155,353 to 329,540.[161] Hispanics now make up 5 percent of the Virginian population. These Hispanic peoples represent people from all regions of Latin America. Some 22 percent of the Hispanics in Virginia are of Mexican origin, another 22 percent come from Central America, 16 percent come from the Caribbean, and 12 percent come from South America.

81

Demographic trends indicate that Hispanic populat
will continue in a similar fashion in the near and distant f
More to the point, the Hispanic population is expected to d
over the next ten years in Virginia. In the greater Richmond are
the Hispanic population has grown by 227 percent in the last ten
years. This represents a growth rate seven times that of the U.S.
population in general. Also notable is the fact that Hispanic pur-
chasing power in Virginia has more than doubled in less that a
decade, from $2.1 billion to over $5.8 billion annually.

Since most of this population is young and recently married, it
represents a significant market and vital workforce for the state.[163]
Its presence is reshaping Virginia into a more inclusive, multicultural, and competitive economy, both nationally and globally.

In 1990, sixty-five residents of Galax City, Virginia, claimed
Hispanic origin. In 2000, the number was 757, a growth rate of
1,065 percent. In fact, if it hadn't been for its Hispanic residents,
Galax City would have lost population. This is just one dramatic
example of the way growth in the Hispanic population reported in
the 2000 Census has changed the face of Virginia in the last
decade. [164]

Though the total percentage of Hispanics in Virginia grew by
only 2 percentage points--from 3 percent in 1990 to 5 percent in
2000--this represents a gain of over 889,000 people, and an
increase of 106 percent in the total Hispanic population. The
increase of slightly over 169,000 Hispanic people represents 19
percent of the state's total gain of 889,318 people.[165] The tremendous gains in numbers of people make attention to Hispanic
ministries imperative.

The Hispanic Churches in Tidewater

Currently, there are sixteen Hispanic churches in Tidewater
affiliated with different denominations as follows: Independent,
Church of God, Assemblies of God, Baptist, Pentecostal Holiness,
and Charismatic churches.[166] The Hispanic congregations gather
less than 2,000 people in all, while it is estimated that twice that
number of Hispanics gather in non-Hispanic evangelical congregations.

in that, at most, only 5 percent of the area's
tly attending an evangelical church. In other
one church for every 300 people who need to
here is a real need for training emerging lead-
ritual need of the Hispanic community in the
area.

I am a member of an intercessory prayer group consisting of
Hispanic pastors and leaders of Tidewater. This group is praying for
at least fifty churches by the year 2014. That means that at least
thirty-six new Spanish-speaking (including some bilingual)
churches must be established.

El Mundo Para Cristo Church of God

I am currently serving as pastor of El Mundo Para Cristo
Church of God as part of my working in the denomination as a
church planter and secretary for the Hispanic Board in the state of
Virginia. The following paragraphs include information about this
church.

- Description of the Ministry

    o Name of the church: "El Mundo Para Cristo Church of
      God" (EMPC)
    o Location: 601 Volvo Parkway, Chesapeake, VA 23320
    o Target Area: Tidewater
    o Families: eleven, Adults: thirty-seven, Youth: nineteen,
      and Children: nineteen
    o Beginning Date: September 2002

- Composition of People and Leadership
    o Core/ leadership Group

        - Seven leaders: two women and five men
        - They also function as Deacons; no Elders yet
        - Sunday school: one leader and three Teachers

83

- Praise and Worship Team: one leader and five singers.
- Missionary couple: one (in process)
- Intercession/ Prayer: one leader
- Discipleship: eight people involved
- Evangelism: to be developed and implemented
- Cell Groups Ministry: three cell groups
- Youth Ministry: one leader in process of organizing the ministry

Countries of Origin
  o Mexico: 37%
  o Ecuador: 22.2%
  o Hispanic-Americans: 15%
  o Colombia: 10%
  o Honduras: 7%
  o Puerto Rico: 2.8%
  o Cuba: 2.8%
  o Venezuela: 2%

- Occupations

  o Field workers
  o Construction workers
  o Military personnel
  o Business people

- Religious Background

  o Most nominal Catholics in country of origin
  o Baptist
  o Evangelical
  o Fundamentalist
  o Charismatic

In regards to multiethnic leadership, I currently have seven people in the core group of EMPC Church of God: one of them is Colombian, two are Puerto Ricans, two are Mexicans, one is Venezuelan, and another one is from the USA. The composition of the core group is diverse, and they have different educational and occupational backgrounds. One leader is involved in the construction business. Three persons hold a doctoral degree in different fields. There are two persons who are currently pursuing an M.A. (one in missions and the other one in education). One person holds a medical technology degree, and I am currently a doctorate candidate of the D. Min. program at Regent University.

People interested in evangelizing the Hispanic population for Christ should recognize the following points in order to be most effective in their outreach. These lessons were important elements that I considered during the development and implementation phases of this D.Min. Project.

- Hispanics are here to stay.

- Hispanics are bringing their families from their countries of origin.

- Hispanics tend to identify with what mainstream Americans regard as "traditional values."

- Religion and family are essential in their culture.

- Hispanics are fascinated by their language, customs, music, and recognized personalities (authors, praise and worship leaders, musicians, known Hispanic pastors, etc).

The Hispanic Leadership Certificate Program

The Hispanic Leadership Certificate Program was planned and implemented for this D.Min. project to provide nonacademic training for pastors and emerging leaders in the Hispanic community in the Tidewater region. The author designed the curriculum according to the recommendations of the pastors of the area.

The author has been involved with the Hispanic community for more than seven years. He organized thirteen different all-day training workshops for community leaders through the ministry of Semilla (Latin American Leadership Program headquartered at Regent University) and Tidewater for Christ project. These experiences have enabled the author to identify the some of the needs for effective training that will enable pastors and emerging leaders to bless their communities more effectively.

The following is the list of topics that the Tidewater for Christ project covered over four years during the all-day training workshops for the Hispanic community: 1) Analysis of the Hispanics in Tidewater, (2) strategies to reach out the Hispanics in Tidewater area, (3) enriching the devotional life of the leader, (4) understanding God's will in our times, (5) Christian education and the church, (6) the importance of networking and spiritual covering, (7) the burnout and stress in ministry, (8) mobilization for the harvest, (9) retaking the weapons of prayer and intercession, (10) stewardship as a whole in the life of the leader, (11) overcoming the depression, (12) walking on God's freedom, and (13) Biblical principles of government.

This process through the "Tidewater for Christ" project was the platform that God used in my ministry to realize the urgent need for training among the Hispanic community. I encouraged and inspired Hispanic pastors, missionaries and emerging leaders so that they will continue expanding God's kingdom in every community that they have been called to serve.

I met with Dr. Sergio Matviuk, the director of the Center for Latin American Studies (CLAL) in the School of Leadership at Regent University, to share about the needs of the Hispanic Community. We began to pray for the possibility of partnering with Regent University. After several meetings, Dr. Matviuk received the approval from the Dean of the School of Leadership. From our meetings, Regent University agreed to partner and network to establish and implement the Hispanic Leadership Certificate Program (HLCP).

In order to establish effective communication, I updated the database of the Hispanic pastors in Tidewater. This allowed me to correspond with these leaders via emails and phone calls to share my heart with them of the need of training emerging Hispanic Christian leaders and pastors in Virginia, and how this project could be an answer for the lack of access to adequate ministerial training.

The electronic communication allowed me to also inform Hispanic Christian leaders and pastors about surveys and meetings. Through a series of meetings with pastors, I gathered valuable input from these leaders. During the meetings, I had the opportunity to present the goals and purpose of this program, and they were supportive of the plan.

I was interested in analyzing both the reality and tendencies of the involvement of the Hispanics in terms of theological education. I conducted a survey in the Tidewater area of the Hispanic pastors and leaders from different denominations to evaluate some of their perceptions and expectations in regard to the model and characteristics of the Hispanic Leadership Program.

I included in the survey questions about their preferences for length, model, and kind of program. Based on the survey's results, I designed the curriculum (nonformal) to organize the Hispanic Leadership Certificate Program. I also included key questions that were oriented to find out the current situation and the expectations from the pastors, and also to have a better understanding of the type of model and methodology for the leadership certificate.

Subsequently, I evaluated the survey's results and found some key elements that led me in the right direction in terms of the initiation and development of the Leadership Certificate Program. The input that I got from this survey was essential for the development of this project. It needs to be contextualized according to the real needs of the community. After the initial deliberation and approval of my ministry project, I came up with a project design of putting together the model and curriculum for the pilot program.

I chose the methods for the training based upon the results from the survey among the pastors. I paid special attention to the changes that were needed and was sensitive to the recommendations from the local pastors and leaders.

I promoted and scheduled the Leadership Certificate Program among the Hispanic churches and ministries in the area by using different methods, such as emails, phone calls, and personal meetings. Based on the enthusiastic response in the immediate region, I began to promote the program among the Hispanic-churches of the Church of God in Virginia.

I wrote the goals and purpose of the Hispanic Leadership Certificate Program. This was a learning process to me because I realized the importance of establishing adequate and realistic goals for the program.

I also prepared the budget to include the expenses required for the project. This budget was based on twenty to twenty-five students. The total budget needed was $11,000. I also wrote a proposal to raise the funds for the project. Several churches and ministries responded favorably to help fund the program. The following lists contain the details.

- Budget
    - o Regent University (CLAL) contributed $15,000
    - o The remaining budget for the HLCP (four courses) was $11,000
    - o Overhead expenses = $1,000
    - o Administration of the program = $800
    - o Salary for four instructors = $3,200 ($800 per class)

- Tuition
    - o The overall cost of the tuition program was $500 per student.
    - o With special arrangements with Regent, CLAL (Dr. Sergio Matviuk), and Administration, three installments were allowed ($200 and two at $150).
    - o The program's $11,000 costs were paid recovered by student payments.

- Funding for Scholarships
    - o Parkway Temple donated $600 for scholarship fund.
    - o Vida Entertainment (Ray Horowitz) donated $500 for scholarship fund.
    - o Dr. Joseph Umidi, TLC, donated $500 for scholarship fund.
    - o Rev. Brian Fields donated $500 for the administration of the program.
    - o The total amount received for the scholarship fund was $1,600.

I finalized all the details with Dr. Matviuk and began to partner and network with the CLAL to implement the Leadership Certificate Program. Regent agreed to offer to the students who finished the program four Continuing Education Units (CEU).

I also prepared an application form that the students completed as part of the registration process for the HLCP. Before the initiation of the program, the students filled out an "entrance student profile" questionnaire that consisted of seventeen questions (Likert-type scale). Upon completion of the program, approximately two months later, participants completed the same questionnaire at the end of the pilot program.

I implemented the pilot program (two courses) including the elaboration of a student profile (pre and post) to evaluate the results of the project. This was one of the ways that I used to evaluate the results of the program.

I reported periodically to my field mentors, dissertation committee, and the Church of God leaders. I was interested in growing in every area of my life through this process. This process was a powerful journey of faith with the Lord to bless the body of Christ. I pray that our Lord will use what He taught me while I was on this journey.

The Model of the HLCP

The model is nonformal theological training. It is practical oriented rather than academic focused. The target group is young-adults (20-36 years old) who have a heart for ministry and need to be trained to better serve the Lord.

The Leadership Certificate Program followed the model of cohort. This approach facilitated the process of spiritual growth by working together in one accord. The Hispanic community is relational, and even though the participants were using the Blackboard system to post their dialogues, they sustained a sense of relationship throughout the pilot program.

The pilot program consisted of two courses (nonformal education). Each course lasted four weeks. During the first week of each course (Saturday), the students came to Regent campus for orientation, where they received adequate instructions to allow them to begin the first course.

During the following three weeks (post-session dialogue in Blackboard), the students were encouraged to participate and post their dialogues in the Spanish language, including interactions with

cohort members by using the Blackboard System. I taught the fii.
class (LH101) and Dr. Marcela Matviuk taught the second class
(LH102). The assignments, plan of the courses, and timeline were
followed as planned at the beginning of the pilot program.

The learning activities included in the courses are the following:
panel discussions, power point presentations, audio-visuals, classroom discussion, small group interaction and strategizing, case
studies, guest speakers, etc. (See the schedule of the program
below).

Hispanic Leadership Certificate Program

HLCP promotes and facilitates practical training for Hispanic
leaders, pastors, and missionaries who want to impact God's world
through the Gospel of Jesus Christ (Eph. 4:11-12). It is the intention of this program to find, contextualize, and utilize relevant
resources and materials to equip emerging leaders to better serve
their communities where God has called them.

Program Objectives

This section describes the HLCP program objectives. They are
in list format to allow the reader to more easily and grasp the con-
cepts of the program.

- Knowledge:
  - Biblical and Theological
    - Understanding of God, man, church, unity and
      love
    - To understand the nature of God's calling in life
  - Cultural
    - To be aware of different subcultures among the
      Hispanic community

Sociological

- o To understand the value of learning in order to promote the welfare of Hispanic families
- o To promote education among both men and women among the Hispanics

- Attitudes

  - o Character
    - o To experience acceptance among other culture groups
    - o To better understand our identity in Christ
    - o To foster passionate spirituality
  - o Attitudes and feelings
    - o To be able to accept people from various cultures
    - o To be able to recognize the diversity and the values of unity

- Perceptions (worldviews)

  - o To recognize the unique contribution of every ethnic group to society
  - o To walk in God's freedom
  - o To identify our weaknesses by allowing the Holy Spirit to work in our lives
  - o To respect other peoples' viewpoint
  - o To increase our level of integrity and ethics in ministry

- Skills

  - o To develop competency in computers and English (ESL, GED).
  - o To be able to relate with people in authority
  - o How do I respond to crisis?
  - o How do I manifest victory?

Every ethnic group contributes to society

HLCP Course Descriptions

This section describes the two courses included in the HCLP program. The classes were Biblical Principles of Leadership & The Purpose of Leadership.

Biblical Principles of Leadership:
Description and Purpose

Course Title: Biblical Principles of Leadership (LH101)

Instructor: Rev. Victor H. Cuartas

This is the first course of the HLCP program, and it focuses on Biblical principles that show us how Jesus was able to exercise leadership principles. The students will be able to identify some weaknesses and strengths in their lives so that they can look at Jesus' model of leadership.

- Key aspects:
  - ○ Looking at Jesus as a leader
  - ○ The issue of the heart
  - ○ Establishing priorities
  - ○ Understanding God's timing
  - ○ Recognizing our limitations

- Program Competencies
  - ○ Recognizes and follows Jesus' example of leadership
  - ○ Recognizes both strengths and weaknesses

Purpose of Leadership:
Description and Purpose

Course Title: The Purpose of Leadership (LH102)

Instructor: Dr. Marcela Matviuk de Chavan

This course will present important characteristics of leadership in order to fulfill the purpose of the program. The students will be able to compare the characteristics between today's tendencies in leadership and the real purpose of leadership based on the Scriptures.

- Key Aspects:
  - o God's purpose in our lives
  - o You are special for God
  - o Understanding the nature of belonging
  - o Everything has a time
  - o We are God's vessels

- Program Competencies
  - o Understands God's will and call
  - o Conducts life with balance
  - o Eager for spiritual renewal in self and others

Program Competencies

1. Recognizes and follows Jesus' example of leadership
2. Understands God's will and call
3. Focuses on God's mission in ministry
4. Conducts life with balance
5. Recognizes both strengths and weaknesses
6. Walks along others in accountability
7. Eager for spiritual renewal in self and others

Participants in HLCP

Twenty-two students were registered for the Hispanic Leadership Pilot Program. There were five churches represented, and the students were divided in three groups according to similarities, level of education, and basic information that I obtained, from the application forms that the students completed at the beginning of the program.

The cohort was diverse and unique. The students came from different backgrounds and levels of leadership. The program was designed with flexibility in terms of the model. The students from Gainesville, Virginia, and Alexandria, Virginia, came to the Regent campus only for the program orientation. The students also were encouraged to post at least two dialogues per week through the Blackboard system.

At the end of each class, during the fourth week, the students were asked to write a practical paper (two the three pages in length) in which they applied key principles that they learned during the class. Most of the Hispanics work hard and they have busy schedules; therefore the two courses designed were practical oriented.

The build-up of the sessions went according to people's needs, as well as the methodology that was implemented. The students were asked to come to Regent Campus just for the orientation and LH101 modular class. The instructor of LH102 traveled to Gainesville, Virginia and taught during the modular session (an eight hour-class).

Profile of the Hispanic Pastors and Leaders in Virginia

I conducted a survey in Gainesville, Virginia of thirty-one Hispanic pastors and leaders. With the growing of the Hispanic population in Virginia, I believe there is a growing need to equip pastors and leaders for the ministry. The following are the results of the survey that gave us an idea of the profile of the Hispanic pastors and leaders in Virginia.

Background and General Information

The surveyed pastors and leaders in Gainesville were from seven countries in Latin America: Colombia (29 percent), El Salvador (23 percent), Venezuela (19 percent), Bolivia and Mexico (10 percent each), Guatemala (6 percent), and Chile (3 percent).[167] The average number of years in ministry was 6.5, and the median age of the group was 40 years. The youngest person surveyed was twenty-six years old, and the oldest person was fifty-seven years old. In terms of gender, the representation in the survey was similar; sixteen male and fifteen female. Fifty-two percent of the respondents were married, 42 percent were single, and 6 percent were widows.[168]

Denominational Background

The Table 3 shows the denominational background of the respondents. A total of five churches were represented, and 72 percent of the surveyed pastors and leaders came from independent churches. In general, there was a positive response from the Hispanic pastors for attaining theological training. Usually, the mainline denominations have their own programs for training their leaders and pastors. On the contrary, the independent churches have limited access for theological training.

These data confirm that an approach to ministerial training in an approach that is cross-denominational is a substantial need in the Hispanic community. This need can be partially met in an model such as presented in this book.

Table 3

Denominational Background of the Respondents

Denomination	Number	Percent
Independent	22	72
Church of God	6	19
Ekklesia USA	2	6
Baptist	1	3
Total	**31**	**100**

Note: See Appendix 4-D for details.

Levels of Education

Table 4 summarizes the education attainment of the respondents. The surveyed pastors and leaders in Gainesville had not attained higher levels of education. Only 10 percent have master's degrees and just 3 percent have a doctorate degree. Twenty-two percent of the respondents did not finish high school for different reasons.

These findings emphasize the urgent need for promoting and implementing new strategies for theological training among Hispanics. However, there is a strong desire among the pastors and leaders for improving their level of education and training for the ministry; the respondents were asked to write their preferences in regard to the highest level of education that they wanted to attain in the future.

Their preferences were remarkable: (1) 56 percent wanted to attain a doctorate degree, (2) 19 percent a master's degree, and (3) 19 percent wanted to attain a bachelor's degree.[169] From this sample, one can infer that there is an increasing awareness for the need for training among Hispanic pastors and leaders. Therefore, there is a tremendous potential for developing and implementing new models for theological training.

Table 4

**Level of Education of
Hispanic Pastors and Leaders in Gainesville**

Level of Education	Number	Percent
Elementary Completion	4	13
Up to 8th Grade	1	3
9th-11th Grade	2	6
High School Completion	19	62
Community College	1	3
Master Degree	3	10
Doctorate/ Ph. D	1	3
Total	31	100

Note: See Appendix 4-E for details.

Motivations for Attaining Theological Training

The following are the respondents' preferences regarding the most important motivations for attaining theological training: (1) to know more about the Bible, (2) to improve their knowledge of the Bible, (3) to better serve in the local churches, (4) to identify their spiritual gifts, and (5) to improve their devotional life. Based on the respondents' preferences, there is a passionate desire from them to know more about the Scriptures and to be able to better serve in their communities where God has called them.[170] Table 5 summarizes the major obstacles to study and the favorite fields of study of the respondents.[171]

As can be seen from this table, the main obstacles for attaining theological education are the lack of finances and the lack of time for enrolling in the institutions fulltime. The responses, albeit from a small sample from a single geographic area, may be indicative of the increasing awareness among the Hispanic community to implement fundraising strategies as well as create new models for theological training that will allow the participants to continue in their ministries while they are pursuing theological training (modular classes, Blackboard system, etc).

Table 5

Obstacles among Hispanics for
Attaining Theological Education

Major Obstacles to Study	Favorite Fields of Study
1. Finances	1. Teaching and doctrine
2. Lack of Time (limitations)	2. Leadership
3. Lack of English Proficiency	3. Counseling
4. Full Time Ministry	4. Christian Education
5. Inadequate Programs of study	5. Evangelism
6. Lack of information	6. Discipleship

Computer Competency

The survey shows that 77 percent of the respondents have a computer at home and 23 percent do not. Even though most of the respondents have a computer at home, only 23 percent of the respondents have advanced computer skills. The findings also show that 74 percent of the respondents have access to the Internet. From this sample, one can assume that there is a need for improving computer competency among Hispanic pastors and leaders. This information helped me to schedule basic computer classes for the students, prior the initiation of the Hispanic Leadership Certificate Program at Regent University.[172]

Profile of the HLCP Students

The twenty-two students who registered for the HLCP were asked to complete an application form that included background information, computer competency, English proficiency, education attainment, and personal references. Participants were also asked to sign a personal contract.[173] This information given by the students was important to understand the profile of the Hispanic pastors and leaders that enrolled in the HLCP. [174]

Background and General Information

The summary of the HLCP students' profile has been included.[175] One of the most important elements of this program was the diversity of the participants' background. The participants of the HLCP represented nine countries: Colombia (36.4 percent), El Salvador (22.7 percent), Honduras (9.1 percent), Mexico (9.1 percent), Panama (4.5 percent), Guatemala (4.5 prcent), Peru (4.5 percent), Ecuador (4.5 percent), and Puerto Rico (4.5 percent).[176] The students from Colombia and El Salvador together represented 58.1 percent of the participants of the HLCP. The median age of the group was thirty years. The age range of the participants was twenty-one to fifty-eight.

Ninety percent of the students were married, and there were a total of 4 married couples in the program.[177] There were 10 males (45.5 percent) and 12 females (54.5 percent) enrolled in the program.[178]

Table 6 summarizes the place of residence of the students in the Commonwealth of Virginia. The HLCP had a total of fourteen students from the Alexandria-Gainesville, Virginia area and eight students from Tidewater.[179] One of the remarkable facts about this program is that the students were so willing to travel for the orientation of the program and on-campus sessions (LH101 and LH102) that were held at Regent University. Most of the students drove for nine hours (roundtrip) to attend the Saturday session.

Table 6

Places of Residence of the HLCP's Students

Place	Number	Percent
Virginia Beach	5	22
Gainesville	4	18
Manassas	4	18
Sterling	2	9
Centreville	2	9
Haymarket	2	9
Chesapeake	1	5
Portsmouth	1	5
Norfolk	1	5
Total	**22**	**100**

Denominational Background

A total of five Hispanic churches were represented in the program, and 68.2 percent the students came from independent churches. The Church of God and Baptist denominations were also represented.[180] There is a lot of potential for this program because there are approximately sixteen Hispanic churches in Tidewater that can be blessed by sending their emerging leaders for training.[181] Table 7 summarizes this information.

Table 7

Summary of the Denominational Background of HLCP Students

Denomination	Number	Percent
Independent	15	68.2
Church of God	6	27.3
Baptist	1	4.5
Total	**22**	**100**

Levels of Education

Table 8 summarizes the education attainment of the students. The table shows that the most participants have not completed much education at the postsecondary level; just 18.2 percent have spent some years in community college, and only 22.7 percent have bachelor's degrees. It is important to note that none of the students have graduate degrees.[182] However, 95.5 percent of the students completed high school. This shows tremendous progress in comparison with the Hispanic survey conducted by this writer, which shows that 22 percent of the respondents did not finish high school. Obviously, much work remains regarding education among Hispanics.

Table 8

Education Attainment of HLCP Students

Level of Education	Number	Percent
9th-12th Grade	1	4.5
High School Completion	12	54.6
Community College	4	18.2
Bachelor's Degree	5	22.7
Master's Degree	0	0
Total	22	100

Computer Competency

Table 9 describes the computers' competency of the students. Only 18 percent of the students had advanced computer skills prior to the initiation of the HLCP.[183] As we observed from the table, 27 percent of the students had poor computer skills, and this limitation was a challenge for some of the students because they had to use the Blackboard system and send emails to their professors and classmates.

To meet this need, the students received basic computer training before the program so that they could fulfill the requirements of the program. At the end of the program, all the students improved their computer skills. Efforts such as this training must give attention to the needs of many students to increase their skills with computers and other electronic equipment.

Table 9

Summary of Computer Competency of HLCP Students

Computer Competency	Number	Percent
Poor	6	27
Basic	12	55
Advanced	4	18
Total	**22**	**100**

Ministry Involvement

The cohort for the HLCP consisted of three pastors, two pastors' wives, and seventeen lay people. Out of the seventeen lay people, thirteen of them were actively involved in their churches prior the initiation of the HLCP.[184] Obviously, the cohort was directly involved in the ministries of the churches.

Evaluation of the Project

The process followed to evaluate the project was the following:

1. I conducted periodic reviews during the research, meetings and interviews throughout the entire process of the ministry project.

2. I evaluated the information and the input received as a result of the fieldwork. All the information was filed and organized according to the distinctive areas in progress.

3. I conducted a survey among the Hispanic pastors

and leaders. The information was processed and evaluated following the statistical parameters needed. I used the statistical software to analyze MSExcel.

4. I searched the updated information from the U.S. Census Bureau, in order to find the latest census data regarding the Hispanic-American population in the USA. These statistics helped me to evaluate the impact of the Hispanics in this nation.

5. I initiated and developed the Hispanic Leadership Certificate Program in the Tidewater area.

6. Then, I wrote and organized a "Student Profile" as a main resource for evaluating the progress of this project during the phase of implementation. At the end of the program, the students were asked to fill out an evaluation form in the Internet. The responses were anonymous so that they can evaluate both classes (LH101 and 102) with liberty.

7. The assessment of this project was focused on the students' impact of the program regarding their behavior and understanding of Jesus' model of leadership. I selected two HLCP students at random and interviewed them and asked ten-qualitative questions to evaluate the results of the pilot program. The questions that I included in the interview helped me to assess the impact that the pilot program had on the leadership skills of the students based on Biblical principles and Jesus' model of leadership.

I believe that this project is important because it will assist in the problem of not having relevant theological training among the Hispanic Americans. This project will provide an important alternative as a model for training emerging leaders for the work of the ministry. The main result of the Doctor of Ministry project will be the final approved dissertation, but God's process in this journal of faith is the paramount purpose.

Summary of Chapter Four

This chapter included a detailed description of the HLCP in Tidewater area. The context of the project is the Hispanic population in the Commonwealth of Virginia.

The background of this project made clear the urgent need for nonformal theological training among Hispanics. A total of twenty students were registered for the HLCP and the target group was young-adults (20-36 years old) who had a heart for the ministry. The program was successfully developed and can be replicated according to the background of the students and the emphasis in the curriculum content needed. The curriculum was designed according to the recommendations of the pastors and leaders of the area. The program followed the cohort model and nonformal theological training.

CHAPTER 5

RESULTS, IMPLICATIONS, CONTRIBUTIONS, AND FUTURE WORK

When I started this project, there was a desire in my heart to understand the characteristics for developing a model to train Hispanic pastors and emerging leaders for the ministry. The results of this process convey the contributions of the HLCP to the Hispanic leaders and pastors in Virginia. The insights that I gained from this process helped me to implement this project.

This chapter describes the analysis of the results of the two-month pilot program that was implemented. In addition, the chapter will include some implications of the results and present several suggestions about the future work on training Hispanic pastors and leaders for the ministry. I believe that this project is important because it will assist in overcoming the problem of not having relevant theological training among Hispanic Americans.

Results from the Project

In this section I will describe Pre- and Post- Student Profile, the online survey evaluation of HLCP courses, and the Blackboard Statistics. Then, I will present the results of the Participants' Grades as well as the Random Interviews of two participants. Finally, I will show some limitations to consider in this pilot project.

HLCP Pre- and-Post Student Profile

Table 10 summarizes the comparative evaluation scores of the students' profile made by the participants before and after the HLCP (two months later).[185] As shown by this table, the total score of the cohort (including 16 questions) before the program was 1,614 and total score after the program was 1,657. There is generally a positive increase of 43 points. The lowest score before the HLCP was 61 (80 is the maximum possible per question) and the highest score was 80. The lowest score after the HLCP was 65, and the highest score was 79.

Table 10
Comparative Results of the Student Profile
Before and After the HLCP

Name	Score Before	Score After
ST1	75	79
ST2	74	68
ST3	78	79
ST4	76	79
ST5	77	78
ST6	76	76
ST7	76	75
ST8	74	68
ST9	78	70
ST10	74	79
ST11	77	79
ST12	68	77
ST13	65	79
ST14	61	74
ST15	76	76
ST16	74	74
ST17	76	73
ST18	61	65
ST19	80	76
ST20	71	76
ST21	72	78
ST22	75	79
Total	**1614**	**1657**

The above findings showed that there was a general improvement in the understanding and perception of the leadership model according to Jesus' example after the HLCP. The assessment was focused on the understanding and knowledge of Jesus' model of leadership. In general, all the students showed an improvement regarding their effort to follow Jesus' example of leadership.

Nevertheless, in addition to finding the total scores, I decided to calculate the mean and the median along with other statistical findings to better understand the contributions of the HLCP. Table 11 shows that the mean before the program was 73.4 and the mean after the program was 75.3. Therefore, there is an average positive increase of 1.9 points for the participants after the HLCP.

The summary of statistical results before and after the HLCP, however, contained in Tables 10 and 11, does not yet convey whether or not it is statistical significant.[186] For that reason, I used a t-test to calculate a t-score for two correlated samples, since the sample size in the project was less than the required number (usually more than 35), the data was insufficient to produce valid statistics. Therefore, I decided to disregard the results the t-test. Another reason for the results in this sample was the fact that many students were already in leadership positions before they began the HLCP, so the difference in the students' profile before and after the HLCP was not significant.

Online Survey Evaluation of HLCP Courses

In order to assess the contributions of the HLCP, the students were asked to complete an online evaluation regarding their development of leadership skills based on Jesus' model of leadership. The titles of the classes in the program were biblical.

Table 11
Statistical Results Before and
After the HLCP

Item	Data Before	Data After
SUM	1614	1657
Mean	73.4	75.3
Standard Error	1.1	1
Median	75	76
Range	19	14
Minimum	61	65
Maximum	80	79
Variance (S²)	27	17.3
Standard Deviation	5.2	4.2
Coefficient of Variation	7%	5.5%

Note: $N = 22$; Range, 16-80.

Principles of Leadership (LH01) and Purpose of Leadership (LH102).[187]

The evaluation survey consisted of eleven questions. Thirteen students answered the online survey for LH101; fourteen students completed the online survey for LH102.[188]

I included the Likert-type scale technique in the surveys that were administered at the end of LH101 and LH102. The surveys contained a set of attitude statements to measure the under-standing of Biblical principles and the improvement of leadership skills of the participants. Subjects were asked to express agree-ment or disagreement on a five-point scale. Each degree of agreement was given a numerical value from one to five. Thus, a total numerical value can be calculated from all the responses.

On a scale of one to five, the students indicated their level of agreement or disagreement to eleven questions based on the following options:

(1) Strongly Disagree, (2) Disagree, (3) Neutral, 4) Agree, and (5) Strongly Agree. The online evaluation survey completed by the participants helped me to assess their understanding of the biblical principles for leadership as well as their improvement in their abilities of leadership.[189]

Table 12 summarizes the statistical results of the online evaluation for LH101. Table 12 shows the mean was 52.9 and the median was 54, which is high keeping in mind that the highest score possible was 55 (eleven questions multiplied for five points maximum per question). The total percentage of the cohort was 96.2, which means that the participants improved their under-standing of Jesus' model of leadership and their leadership skills. Note that *all* the 13 participants marked "strongly agree" when asked whether the LH101 class increased their expectation regarding to their own leadership.[190]

Table 12

**Statistical Results of the Online
Evaluation for LH101**

Activity		Score
Number of Participants		13
SUM		688
Mean (X)		52.9
Median		54
Maximum Score		55
Total Sum Possible		715
	% Total	96.2

The pilot program also included the evaluation of the LH102 class. Table 13 summarizes the statistical results of the online evaluation for LH102. Thus, it is observed from this table that the results were similar in terms of the efficacy of the program. The mean was 52.8, and the median was 55. The total percentage of the cohort was 96, which one can infer that the program had a positive impact on the participants.

Table 13
Statistical Results of the
Online Evaluation for LH102

Activity	Score
Number of Participants	14
SUM	739
Average/ Mean (X)	52.9
Median	55
Maximum Score	55
Total SUM Possible	770
% Total	96

Out of the 14 participants of the LH102 class, 12 marked "Strongly Agree," but only 2 marked "Agree" on the corresponding question. From these findings, one can infer that the pilot program improved the expectations of the participants regarding their own leadership.

Another important aspect of the results from the online evaluation was the fact that the participants increased their understanding of biblical principles of leadership. As a result, the participants' awareness increased regarding the responsibilities of Christian leaders and their leadership skills as they studied Jesus' model of leadership. Additionally, the students also increased their expectations regarding their own leaders because they analyze the Biblical model of leadership.

Blackboard Statistics for HLCP

The pilot program used the Blackboard (Bb) platform to allow the students to actively participate in every class through responding to three questions every week. Each question asked participants to respond to two reflective comments per question. The LH101 class was offered in Virginia Beach for all the participants. The LH102 class was offered separately in Virginia Beach and Gainesville, Virginia with additional coursework taught online.

This combination of online and in-person coursework proved to be successful, obtaining a record of 100 percent completion rate for the 2005 cohort. The students were divided into three groups according to their background and involvement with their churches. Even though Hispanics are relational, the results of the Bb participation proved that the model of this program met the needs of the participants.[191]

Table 14 shows the summary of the statistics for LH101 Bb. As shown by Table 14, a total of 1,210 hits were received on Bb during the duration of LH101. As seen in the table, the section that received the most responses was course materials and the Bibliography section received the least number of hits. These findings can infer the active participation of the students during LH101.

Table 14
Blackboard Hits for LH101

Folder	Hits	Percent
Course Material	793	65.5
Syllabus	292	24.1
Assignments	84	7.0
External Links	34	2.8
Bibliography	7	0.6
Total	**1,210**	**100**

Note: See Appendix 9-A for details

Table 15 summarizes the students' participation by group during LH102. One explanation for the lower number of hits during the LH102 class is because the participants were more familiar with the Bb system. However, the overall participation of the students was good.

In addition, I also analyzed the students' participation by the three groups in Bb. In general, all three groups had good participation even though the groups did not interact with each other. The initial expectations in terms of participation were different according to the characteristics of each group. For the LH101 Class, Group A consisted of seven students: two pastors and five leaders with a high level of education. Group B consisted of eight

110

students: one associate pastor, one pastor's wife, and six emerging leaders with similar education and background. Group C consisted of seven students who were not actively involved in their churches but had similar backgrounds.

Table 15
Blackboard Hits for LH102

Folder	Hits	%
Course Material	280	50.7
Syllabus	137	24.8
Assignments	123	22.3
Bibliography	8	1.5
External Links	4	.7
Total	**552**	**100**

Note: See Appendix 9-B for details.

Table 16 summarizes the level of the students' participation by the three groups in Bb. As shown by this table, a total of 4,930 were received in Bb from the students. Group C participated most frequently in Bb with 38.2% of the hits. One of the presumptions is that the participants of Group C had more time available to spend in this process. Nevertheless, they showed excellent results and diligence. Group B followed in participation with 31.2 percent, and Group A had 30.6 percent of the total hits received. The results were surprising because Group B had eight students, and the other two had seven students each.

Table 16
Blackboard Participation by
Groups for LH101

Group	Number of Participants	Hits	Percent
A	7	1508	30.6%
B	8	1537	31.2%
C	7	1885	38.2%
Total	**22**	**4,930**	**100%**

For the LH102 class, the groups' participation in Bb was differ-ent; consequently, Table 17 summarizes the students' participation by the groups. It is important to note that for LH102, the groups were reorganized based on the interaction of the participants in LH101, still taking into consideration their backgrounds and level of education. These changes proved to be successful. There were eight participants for Group A, and Groups B and C had seven participants each. After these changes, Table 16 shows that mem-bers in Group A participated most frequently with 39.8 percent of the hits. There was a significant difference in the quality and quantity of responses after all the pastors, pastors' wives and some current leaders were reorganized in Group A. Although Group C participated less; the quality of the participation was good according to their level of education and backgrounds. These find-ings conveyed that the HLCP encouraged the students to actively participate in Bb.

Table 17
Blackboard Participation
by Groups for LH102

Group	Number of Participants	Hits	Percent
A	8	1391	39.8%
B	7	1107	31.7%
C	7	997	28.5%
Total	**22**	**3495**	**100%**

Results of Participants' Grades

The pilot program was successful. All the twenty students fin-ished the pilot program: twenty-one participants successfully passed the two classes, and only 1one participant was not able to pass the LH102 class due to family issues (she did not turn in the final paper). Therefore, the rate of retention of students in the HLCP was 100 percent. The combination of online and in-person coursework met the needs of the participants of the HLCP. At the end of both classes, the participants were required to write practi-cal paper between two and three pages to apply biblical principles of leadership in their context of ministry.

Table 18 summarizes the students' final grades for the HLCP. The minimum score to pass the class was ten points, and the maximum score possible for both classes was fourteen points. As illustrated by this table, the mean score of the participants for LH101 and LH102 was 13.2 and 13.4, respectively. The median of the grades was 13.5 and 14 for LH101 and LH102 respectively.

These results are remarkable because most of the participants were not enrolled in any formal or nonformal method of training for the last five years, and yet they successfully fulfilled all the requirements of the HLCP. A sample of the instructor's progress report for LH101 is included in Appendix 10.

Table 18
Students' Final Grades for
LH101 and LH102

Activity	LH101	LH102
Sum	291.0	295
Average	13.2	13.4
Lowest	12	7
Highest	14	14
Median	13.5	14

Random Interviews of Two Participants

As part of the assessment of the HLCP, two participants (one Peruvian male and one Mexican female) were randomly interviewed. The interview consisted of ten qualitative questions that measure the progress and success of the HLCP.[192] One of the interviewees expressed that at the beginning of the HLCP, she did not see Christ as a leader. Now, after she finished the program, she now depends on Him. According to her, "the Biblical principles of leadership that I have learned really helped me to be more disciplined."

The other interviewee expressed that "This program has transformed my life in such a way that brought awareness of my current situation of leadership by allowing me to recognize both my strengths and weaknesses. My personal life has been blessed because I have improved my discipline in different areas following Jesus' example of leadership." At the personal level, the interviewees were also able to improve their relationship with their children by providing a better example of discipline.

In addition, their level of communication with their spouses improved. One fact that helped the participants during the pilot program was the opportunity that they had to serve their classmates while they were also learning the biblical principles of leadership. When leaders and pastors serve others, they have the opportunity to practice and apply the Biblical principles of leadership. Finally, I want to close with the statement of one of the interviewees,

> My level of commitment with God has increased, as well as my relationship with my family. I am currently planning a mission's trip to my native country Peru; I want to continue gaining more training and will encourage my wife to enroll this program; one of the benefits of this program is that it has brought awareness of the need for working together with my wife by matching our spiritual gifts for the ministry; my burden to serve the Hispanic community has been increased.

Limitations to Consider

This pilot project had several limitations. A significant project limitation was that some of the students were already involved in leadership positions in their churches prior to the initiation of the HLCP. As Christian leaders already, there was not a dramatic increase in leadership understanding of Jesus' model since they already possessed biblical foundations.

Second, the number of students involved in the program did not allow for making calculations that were statistically significant. Normally, thirty-five samples are accepted as the minimum for statistically significant results. Although twenty-two participated in the survey, only thirteen completed the end-of-course survey for LH101 and only fourteen for LH102.

Third, some students had technical problems that limited their participation in Bb because they had old computers. Fourth, this project primarily targeted the first-generation of Hispanics and it needs also to be adjusted to benefit the second and third generations as well. There is a need for bridging the different generations of Hispanics.

Implications and Contributions

I will discuss in this section both the implications and contributions for the Hispanic Churches involved in the HLCP, for "*El Remanente de Dios*" Church, and for *El Mundo Para Cristo* Church of God. In addition, I will also discuss the implications for the Hispanic Pastors and emerging Leaders in Virginia, the Hispanic Pastors and emerging leaders as a whole. Finally, I will conclude describing some implications for this writer.

For the Hispanic Churches Involved in the HLCP

The five churches involved in this project were: First Baptist Church of Norfolk, *Iglesia de Dios Adonai*, *Iglesia de Dios El Mundo Para Cristo*, Rock Church Hispanic Ministry, and *Iglesia El Remanente de Dios*. The leadership team of these churches has been expanded as a result of their involvement in the HLCP. I received the feedback from the pastors, and they are so excited with the improvement of leadership skills of the program participants. Some of the participants are now teaching in their churches, others are more involved in different ministries of their congregations. It is my prayer that these churches will continue supporting and sending other pastors and emerging leaders for theological training.

El Remanente de Dios Church

The environment and dynamics of leadership in this church have drastically changed after the completion of this program. The senior pastor of this church was enrolled in this program along with his wife who is currently leading the praise and worship team and twelve emerging leaders.

As the senior pastor states, "The leadership team of my congregation has been so enriched by this program, and I am already seeing the positive results." He is personally encouraging and modeling the leaders of his own congregation to be trained for effective ministry. It is the intention of this writer to explore some possibilities with Dr. Matviuk (CLAL) to develop more leadership programs for Hispanic pastors and emerging leaders in Virginia. There is also a possibility to offer the HLCP again in the coming years.

El Mundo Para Cristo Church of God

A total of five members of the church that I am currently serving as pastor registered for the HLCP. As a pastor, I can testify that the participants of the program finished with another perspective of leadership. Their attitudes and behaviors have changed for good. They are more willing to serve and follow Jesus' example of leadership. Two members are already actively serving in the praise and worship ministry of our congregation.

There are two ladies who will begin to teach classes to share Biblical principles of leadership with new believers. The church has been blessed by supporting the development of this project. A sense of destiny and a message of God's faithfulness were conveyed throughout the process. This church is fully committed to continue encouraging and supporting emerging leaders to be trained and equipped for the work of ministry.

Hispanic Pastors and Emerging Leaders in Virginia

Approximately sixteen Hispanic churches in the Tidewater a plus several churches in other regions can be blessed by this program. Some of the pastors have already expressed their interest for knowing more about this program. The contributions of the HLCP are great, and this program offers an effective model to train Hispanic pastors and emerging leaders to better serve their communities. There are currently few pastors and leaders in the Hispanic churches with sufficient leadership skills to bless other people. Therefore, it is urgent to continue networking so that we can advance in developing models for theological training.

Hispanic Pastors and Emerging Leaders as a Whole

This writer is concerned about the lack of training among Hispanic pastors and leaders. Hispanics have passion and love to serve the Lord, but unless there is a commitment to train leaders, healthy Hispanic churches won't be established in our midst. The need is great and the harvest is plenty; so the laborers need to be trained to meet the needs of almost 35 million Hispanics in the USA.

Only 20 percent of Hispanics are currently believers, and few pastors and leaders throughout the nation have theological training. This reality conveys the urgent need to support and mobilize the believers and churches for theological training. Hispanic churches can tremendously inspire and support their pastors and emerging leaders to gain training and to follow Jesus' example of leadership as well. As Paul encourages Timothy in his letter: "You then, my son, be strong in the grace that is in Christ Jesus. And the things you have heard me say in the presence of many witnesses entrust to reliable men who will also be qualified to teach others" (2 Tim 2:1-2, KJV).

For the Author

This project is part of God's vision in my life. It has been my heart's desire to develop theological training models to meet the needs of the Hispanic pastors and leaders in Virginia. God has used this project to expand my faith and vision for His kingdom. This process helped me to remember God's promises for my ministry. Now that this pilot program has been developed, I see it as a seed from God that will continue to bless many pastors, missionaries, and ministries.

My colleagues, pastors, and the participants of the HLCP have encouraged me. Thank God for all the ministries and individuals who financially supported this project. The church of God as a whole and my congregation *EMPC* have fully supported me in this process, and this author is convinced that God will continue blessing the Hispanic ministry in the USA and that many unsaved people will become part of God's family.

117

Future Directions

The continuation and expansion of the HLCP is considered to be imperative and necessary. The need for offering the HLCP again and targeting the same audience is obvious. Leaders should determine the tasks of delineating the students' profile according to the requirements and expectations of the program. The potential for leadership training using different methods is tremendous, keeping in mind that Hispanics are the largest minority in this country.

The future is full of hope and promise. Continuing the partnership with CLAL from Regent University and other institutions is imperative in order to develop and implement training programs to meet the needs of the Hispanic communities. I shared this burden for theological training with other leaders and pastors, and I believe that there is going to be an explosion of servant leadership among the Hispanic believers in the USA.

Through the partnership with CLAL and other institutions, different kinds of programs can be developed according to the audiences and specific needs of the churches and communities. Now Hispanic leaders will talk about the "programs of training for the Hispanic pastors and emerging leaders," as Dr. Matviuk expressed during the Commencement Ceremony of the 2005 cohort at Regent University.

In order to continue, this process will require the active involvement and networking of churches, agencies, government organizations, and education institutions to ensure the success of the programs. To develop these programs throughout the United States, it will be necessary to establish an adequate mechanism for fundraising to offer scholarships according to the current needs of the participants. Much more is needed if we want to develop and implement these kinds of programs in Latin American countries.

Concluding Words

This dissertation presents how the author conceived, developed, and evaluated a nonformal Leadership Certificate Program for Hispanic pastors and emerging leaders. The project conveys the urgent need for equipping the future generations that will serve our communities with Biblical principles. Many sources contributed to the conceptualization and development of this project. Some directly cited in this manuscript. However, others were instrumental in this project but not cited.

I hope that God will use this book to bless many pastors and leaders to better serve the Lord through their effective ministries. I am absolutely willing to continue to network and join hands with others for the expansion of God's kingdom. My desire is to be God's vessel so that many can be equipped and respond to God's call to be a blessing for others.

Finally, I am thankful to God for the privilege to enroll and pursue the Doctor of Ministry Program at Regent University. It has blessed my life and my ministry so much, and I am convinced that many people have been blessed already. God is so faithful, and He has given me the strength and grace to finish this process. I desire to continue serving the Lord and His people with love and passion through the power of the Holy Spirit. I will conclude with the words of Paul, who highlighted the importance of preparing people for the ministry:

> And he gave some, apostles; and some, prophets; and some, evangelists; and some, pastors and teachers; For the perfecting of the saints, for the work of the ministry, for the edifying of the body of Christ: Till we all come in the unity of the faith, and of the knowledge of the Son of God, unto a perfect man, unto the measure of the stature of the fullness of Christ (Eph 4:11-13).

Summary of Chapter Five

This chapter described the results, implications, contributions, and future work of the HLCP. The two-month pilot program consisted of two classes: Biblical Principles of Leadership (LH101) and Purpose of Leadership (LH102). The evaluation survey consisted of eleven questions; thirteen students answered the online survey for LH101, and fourteen students completed the online survey for

LH102. The assessment of this project measured the pre- and post-understanding and knowledge of Jesus' model of leadership through student profiles, an online evaluation survey, and random personal interviews.

BIBLIOGRAPHY

Abott, T. K. *The International Critical Commentary.* Edited by R. Driver, A. Plummer, and C. A. Briggs. Edinburgh: T. & T. Clark, 1964.

"Activism Sets SBA Plan in Motion" [article online, 2005]; (accessed 10 June 2005); available from www.hispanicbusiness.com/ newsletter-archive/view.asp?sendoutid=635; Internet.

Allen, Clifton J. ed. *The Broadman Bible Commentary: Matthew-Mark,* vol. 8, *Mark* by Henry Turlington. Nashville: Broadman, 1970

_____. *The Broadman Bible Commentary: Acts-1 Corinthians,* vol. 10. *Acts,* by T. C. Smith. Nashville: Broadman, 1969.

Alessi, Phil. *Biblical Foundations: Barnabas-Gift Oriented Ministry.* Charlottesville, VA: CRM Multiplication Team, 2002.

Alfonso, Regina M. *How Jesus Taught: The Methods and Techniques of the Master.* New York: Alba House, 1986.

Aleshire, Daniel, and Jonathan Strom, ed. Fact Book on Theological Education. Pittsburgh: The Association of Theological Schools, 1996.

Anderson, Allan H. and Walter J. Hollenweger. *Pentecostals After a Century: Global Perspectives on a Movement.* Sheffield, England: Sheffield Academic Press, 1999.

Bakke, Ray. *A Theology as Big as the City.* Downers Grove: InterVarsity, 1997.

Banks, Robert. *Reenvisioning Theological Education: Exploring a Missional Alternative to Current Models.* Grand Rapids: Eerdmans, 1999.

Barker, Kenneth L., and John R. Kohlenberger III. *Zondervan NIV Bible Commentary: New Testament.* Vol. 2. Grand Rapids: Zondervan, 1994.

Barna, George. *Second Coming of the Church. Nashville: Word Books, 1998.*

Barndt Joseph. *Dismantling Racism: The Continuing Challenge to White America.* Minneapolis: Augsburg Fortress, 1991.

Barnes, Albert. *Notes on the New Testament- Ephesians, Philippians, and Colossians.* Edited by Robert Few. Grand Rapids: Baker, 1965.

Beach, Raymond D. "Managerial Leadership Instruction: Assessing Contemporary Seminary Coverage in Light of Biblical Standards." D.Min. diss., Regent University, 1994.

Bernardino, Nomeriano C. "An Effective Training Program in Biblical Preaching for Filipino Pastors in Metro-Manila." D.Min. diss., Regent University, 2002.

BibleWorks 4: The Premier Biblical Exegesis and Research Program. Software for Windows Version 4. Big Fork, MT: 1999.

Blaikie, William Garden. *The Public Ministry of Christ.* Minneapolis: Klock & Klock Christian Publishers, 1984.

Blair, Christine E. "Understanding Adult Learners: Challenges for Theological Education." *Theological Education* 34, no. 1 (1977): 11-24.

Blank, Rodolfo. *Teología y Misión en América Latina.* Saint Louis, MO: Concordia, 1996.

Boaz, Mary. *Teaching at a Distance: A Handbook for Instructors.* Mission Viejo, CA: League for Innovation, 1999.

Bossidy, Larry and Ram Charan. *Execution: The Discipline of getting Things Done.* New York: Crown Business, 2002.

Bowers, Paul., ed. "Evangelical Theological Education Today." Vol. 2, *Agenda for Renewal.* Nairobi: Evangel Publishing, 1982.

Brown, Jeannine K. *The Disciples in Narrative Perspective: The Portrayal and Function of the Matthean Disciples.* Atlanta: Society of Biblical Literature, 2002.

Brown, Ronald Thomas. "Self-leadership and Effective Leadership Behaviors, as Observed by Subordinates." Ph.D. diss., Regent University, 2003.

Bruce, A. B. *The Training of the Twelve: Timeless Principles for Leadership Development.* Grand Rapids: Kregel, 1988.

Brueggemann, Walter. *1 & 2 Kings, Smyth & Helwys Bible Commentary.* Macon, GA: Smyth & Helwys Publishing, 2000.

Calian, Samuel Carnegie. *Where's The Passion for Excellence in the Church? Shaping Discipleship Through Ministry and Theological Education.* Wilton: Morehouse, 1989.

_____. *The Ideal Seminary: Pursuing Excellence in Theological Education.* Louisville, KY: Westminster John Knox, 2002.

Calvin, John. *John Calvin's Sermons on Ephesians.* Translated by Arthur Golding, 1577. Carlisle: Banner of Truth, 1975.

Campbell, Joe Bill, and June Mundy Campbell. *Laboratory Mathematics* 5th ed. St. Louis, MO: Mosby, 1997.

Carter, Milton Dee. "Strengthening Smaller Churches by Mentoring Pastors: The Missouri Pastoral Mentoring Program." D.Min. diss., Regent University, 2002.

Cetuk, Virginia Samuel. *What to expect in a Seminary: Theological Education as Spiritual Formation.* Nashville: Abingdon Press, 1998.

Clarke, W. K. *Concise Commentary on the Whole Bible.* New York: Macmillan, 1953.

Clapp, Rodney. *A Peculiar People: The Church in a Post-Christian Society.* Downers Grove: InterVarsity, 1996.

Clinton, J. Robert. *Clinton's Biblical Leadership Commentary.* Fuller Theological Seminary: 1999.

_____. *Leadership Perspectives: How to Study the Bible For Leadership Insights.* Altadena, CA: Barnabas, 1993.

_____. *The Bible and Leadership Values: A Book by Book Analysis.* Altadena, CA: Barnabas, 1993.

_____. *The Making of a Leader.* Colorado Springs: NavPress, 1988.

Clinton, Bobby, and Laura Raab. *Barnabas, Encouraging Exhorter: A Study in Mentoring.* Altadena, CA: Barnabas, 1997.

Clinton, J. Robert. *"Clinton's Biblical Leadership Commentary."* 1999. Fuller Theological Seminary, CA.

_____. *Having a Ministry That Lasts: Becoming a Bible Centered Leader.* Altadena, CA: Barnabas Publishers, 1997.

_____. *Leadership Series: Conclusion on Leadership Style."* 1992. Fuller Theological Seminary, CA.

_____. *Leadership Training Models.* Altadena: Barnabas, 1984.

Coleman, Robert E. *The Master Plan of Evangelism.* Old Tappan, NJ: Fleming H. Revell Company, 1964.

Collins, Carl A., Jr. *Paul as a Leader: A Study of the Apostle's Role and Influence in the Field of Religious Education.* New York: Exposition, 1955.

Collins, Jim. Good to Great. New York: HarperCollins Publishers, 2001.

Conn, Harvie M., and Samuel F. Rowen, ed. *Missions & Theological Education in World Perspective.* Farmington, MI: Associates of Urbanus, 1984.

Connelly, E. Michael, and D. Jean Clandinin. *Teachers as Curriculum Planers: Narratives of Experience.* New York: Teachers College Press, 1988.

Cox, Harvey. *Fire from Heaven: The Rise of Pentecostal Spirituality and the Reshapingof Religion in the Twenty-Fist Century.* Cambridge, MA: DA Capo, 1995.

Crabb, Larry. *Connecting: A Radical New Vision.* Nashville: Thomas Nelson, Inc. 1997.

Davis, John M. Interview by author, 15 September 2005,Virginia Beach, VA.

Davis, Kenneth G. "The Attraction and Retention of U. S. Hispanics to the Doctor of Ministry Program," *Theological Education* 33, no. 1 (1996): 75-82.

Davis, Kenneth G., and Edwin I. Hernandez. *Reconstructing the Sacred Tower: Challenge and Promise of Latino/a Theological Education*. Scranton, PA: The University of Scranton Press. 2003.

Dawn, Marva and Eugene Peterson. *The Unnecessary Pastor: Rediscovering the Call*. Grand Rapids: Eerdmans, 2000.

Day, Heather F. *Protestant Theological Education in America: A Bibliography*. ATLA Bibliography Series, 15. Metuchen: Scarecrow Press, 1985.

Dearborn, Tim A. *Preparing Leaders for the Future Education . . . Today*. Seattle: Seattle Association for Theological Education, 1995.

Deiros, Pablo y Carlos Mraida. *Latinoamérica en Llamas*. Nashville: Editorial Caribe, 1994.

Dempster, Murray W, Byron D. Klaus, and Douglas Petersen. *The Globalization of Pentecostalism. A Religion Made to Travel*. Irvine, CA: Regnum, 1999.

Dilday, Russell H. *1, 2 Kings, The Communicator's Commentary*. Vol. 9. Waco, TX: Word Books, 1987.

Dickson, Robert Louis. "Qualifications for Presidents, With Application to Theological Seminaries." Ph.D. diss., Regent University, 2000.

Dillon, James T. *Jesus as a Teacher: A Multidisciplinary Case Study*. Bethesda, MD: International Scholars, 1995.

Earle, Ralph, A., and Joseph H. Mayfield. *Beacon Bible Commentary*. Vol. 7. (Kansas City, MO: Beacon Hill, 1965.

Earle, Ralph, A., Elwood Sanner, and Charles L. Childers. *Beacon Bible Commentary*. Vol. 6. Kansas City, MO: Beacon Hill, 1964.

Easton, Lois Brown. *The Other Side of Curriculum: Lessons from Learners*. Portsmouth, NH: Heinemann, 2002.

Eliozondo, Virgilio. *Galilean Journey: The Mexican-American Promise*. Maryknoll, NY: Orbis, 2003.

Espin, Orlando. "The State of U.S. Latino/a Theology: An Understanding."*Hispanic Theological Initiave, Perspectivas: Occasional Papers*. (Fall, 2000): 19-55.

Farley, Edward. *Theologia: The Fragmentation and Unity of Theological Education*. Philadelphia: Fortress, 1983.

Fernández, Eduardo, C. *La Cosecha: Harvesting Contemporary United States Hispanic Theology (1972-1998)*. Collegeville, MN: The Liturgical Press, 2000.

Fernández-Shaw, Carlos M. *The Hispanic Presence in North America from 1492 to Today*, Rev. ed. Translated by Alfonso Bertodan Stourton and others. Facts on File, 1999.

Fernando, Ajith. *Leadership Lifestyle: A Study of I Timothy*. Wheaton, IL: Tyndale House, 1985.

Ferris, Robert W. *Establishing Ministry Training: A Manual for Programme Developers*. Pasadena, CA: William Carey Library, 1995.

_____. *Renewal in Theological Education: Strategies for Change*. Wheaton: Wheaton College Press, 1990.

Figueroa, Allan. *The Second Wave: Hispanic Ministry and the Evangelization of Cultures*. Mahwah, NJ: Paulist Press, 1989.

_____. *Frontiers of Hispanic Theology in the United States*. Maryknoll, NY: Orbis, 1992.

Fletcher, John C. *The Futures of Protestant Seminaries*. Washington, D.C.: Alban Institute, 1983.

Flynn, James T., Wie L. Tjiong, and Russell W. West. *A Well-Furnished Heart: Restoring the Spirit's Place in the Leadership Classroom*. Fairfax, VA: Xulon, 2002.

Foltz, Howard. *Healthy Churches in a Sick World*. Joplin, MO: Messenger Publishing, 1998.

Ford, Leroy. *A Curriculum Design Manual for Theological Education*. Nashville: Broadman Press, 1991.

Foster, Richard J., and James Bryan Smith. *Devotional Classics*. New York: HarperCollins, 1993.

Fox, Geoffrey. *Hispanic Nation: Culture, Politics and the Constructing of Identity.* Secaucus, NJ: Birch Lane Press, 1996.

Franz, Gerald Patrick. "The Compatibility of Practices in American Protestant Seminaries With a Biblical Model of Theological Education." Ph.D., Regent University, 2002.

Freed, Edwin D. *The New Testament: A Critical Introduction.* 3d ed. Stamford: CT, Wadsworth Thompson Learning, 2001.

Gaebelein, Frank E ed. *The Expositor's Bible Commentary: John-Acts.* Vol. 9. Grand Rapids: Zondervan, 1981.

Gangel, Kenneth O. "Delivering Theological Education That Works." *Theological Education* 34 (Autumn 1997): 1-9

Gangel, Kenneth O., and Howard G. Hendricks eds. *The Christian Educator's Handbook on Teaching.* Grand Rapids: Baker, 1988.

Gerber, Michael E. *The E-Myth Revisited.* New York: HarperCollins, 1995.

Gilbert, Sara Dulaney. *How to be a Successful Online Student.* New York: McGraw Hill, 2001.

Godwin, Johnnie C. *Layman's Bible Book Commentary: Mark.* Vol. 16. Nashville: Broadman, 1979.

Goizueta, Roberto S. *Caminemos con Jesús: Toward Hispanic/ Latino Theology of Accompaniment.* Maryknoll, NY: Orbis, 1995.

_____. *Mañana: Christian Theology from Hispanic Perspective.* Nashville: Abingdon Press, 1990.

González, Juan. *A History of Latinos in America: Harvest of Empire.* New York: Penguin Group, 2000.

_____. *The Theological Education of Hispanics.* Atlanta: The Fund of Theological Education, 1988.

González, Justo. *Christian Theology from a Hispanic Perspective.* Nashville: Abingdon, 1990.

Goodwin, Melody Louise Humphries. "The Sister to Sister Mentoring Program." D.Min. diss., Regent University, 2000.

Goodwin, Thomas. *An Exposition of Ephesians*, Chapter 1 to 2:10. Vol. I. *n.p.* Sovereign Grace Book Club, 1958.

Grant, Frederick C. *Nelson's Bible Commentary: New Testament, Matthew-Acts.* Vol. 6. New York: Thomas Nelson & Sons, 1962.

Grigg, Viv. *Cry of the Urban Poor.* Monrovia, CA: MARC, 1992.

Guder, Darrell L., ed. The Missional Church: Grand Rapids: Eerdmans, 1998.

Gulbronson, Thomas Francis. "Models of Renewal for the Twenty-first Century: A Training Program for Developing Mature Churches." D.Min. diss., Regent University, 2001.

Guthrie, Donald. *The Apostles.* Downers Grove: InterVarsity, 1990.

_____. New Testament Introduction. Grand Rapids: Zondervan, 1975.

Harmon, Nolan B., ed. *The Interpreter's Bible: Acts-Romans.* Vol. 9. (Nashville: Abingdon Press, 1954), 73.

Harris, Leslie. Interview by author, 19 January 2005, Hampton, VA.

Hart, D. G. and R. Albert Mohler, Jr., and Bruce K. Waltke, eds. *Theological Education in the Evangelical Tradition.* Grand Rapids: Baker Books, 1996.

Hayslett, H. T. Jr. Statistics Made Simple. New York: Doubleday, 1968.

Henry, Carl F., ed., *The Biblical Expositor: Matthew to Revelation* 2d ed. Vol. 3. Philadelphia: Holman, 1960.

Henry, Matthew. *Concise Commentary on the Whole Bible.* Nashville: Thomas Nelson, 1997.

Hernandez, Edwin, Kenneth Davis, and Catherine Wilson. "The National Survey of Hispanic Theological Education," *Journal of Hispanic/Latino Theology* 8: no. 4 (2001): 37-59.

_____. "The Theological Education of U. S. Hispanics," *Theological Education* 38: no. 2 (2002): 71-85.

Heuser, Roger and Norman Shawchuck. *Leading the Congregation: Caring for Yourself While Serving Others.* Nashville: Abingdon Press, 1993.

Hobbs, T. R. *2 Kings, Word Biblical Commentary,* Vol. 13. Waco, TX: Word Books, 1985.

Hopkins, Jack W. *Latin America: Perspectivas on a Region.* New York: Holmes & Meier, 1998.

Horne, Herman H. *Teaching Techniques of Jesus: How Jesus Taught.* Grand Rapids: Kregel, 1978.

Hough, Jr. Joseph C. and John B. Cobb, Jr. *Christian Identity and Theological Education.* Chico: Scholars, 1985.

House, Paul R. *1, 2 Kings, The New American Commentary.* Vol. 8. Nashville, TN: Broadman & Holman, 1995.

Isasi Ada Maria and Fernando F. Segovia. *Hispanic/Latino Theology: Challenge and Promise.* Minneapolis: Fortress Press, 1996.

Johns, Timothy Mac. "Restoration of the Spiritual Family as an Emerging Apostolic Paradigm." D.Min. diss., Regent University, 2002.

Johnson, Spencer. *Who Moved My Cheese? An Amazing Way to Deal with Change in Your Work and Life.* Schuster and Schuster Audio Books, 1998.

Johnston, Jay, and Ronald K. Brown. *Teaching the Jesus Way: Building a Transformational Teaching Ministry.* Nashville: Lifeway, 2000.

Johnstone, Patrick and Jason Mandryk. *Operation World: The Day-to-Day Guide to Praying for the World.* Grand Rapids: Zondervan Publishing House, 2001.

_____. *Operation World: When We Pray God Works.* 21st Century Edition. Pasadena, CA: WEC International, 2001.

Jones, J. D. *The Apostles of Christ.* Minneapolis: Klock & Klock, 1982.

Kanellos, Nicolas, ed. *The Hispanic-American Almanac: A Reference Work on Hispanics in the United States* 2nd ed. Gale, 1997.

Karris, Robert J. *The Collegeville Bible Commentary: New Testament.* (Collegeville, MN: The Liturgical Press, 1992.

Kelsey, David H. *Between Athens and Berlin: The Theological Education Debate.* Grand Rapids: Eerdmans, 1993.

Kelsey, David H. and Barbara G. Wheeler. The ATS Basic Issues Research Project: Thinking about Theological Education. *Theological Education* 30, no. 2 (Spring 1994): 71-80.

Kemp, Jerrold E. The Instructional Design Process. New York: Harper and Row, 1985.

Kinsler, F. Ross. The Extension Movement in Theological Education. South Pasadena: William Carey Library, n.d.

Kim, Andrew. "A Basic Training Manual for Cell-based Church Interns." D.Min. diss., Regent University, 2002.

Kimball, John Richard. "Mobilizing Bethlehem Congregational Church: A Critical Study on Missions Mobilization within a Small Church of the Conservative Congregational Christian Conference (Virginia)." D.Min. diss., Regent University, 2001.

Kopp, O. W. *Personalized Curriculum through Excellence in Leadership.* Danville, IL: The Intersate Printers & Publishers, 1974.

Kraft, Charles H. Christianity and Culture. Maryknoll, NY: Orbis, 1979.

_____. *Communicating Jesus' Way.* Pasadena, CA: William Carey Library, 1998.

Kraft, Charles, and Mark White, eds. *Behind Enemy Lines: An Advanced Guide to Spiritual Warfare.* Ann Arbor, MI: Vine Books, 1994.

Lau, Linda. *Distance Learning Technologies: Issues, trends, and Opportunities.* Hershey, PA: Idea Group, 2000.

Law, Eric H. F. *The Wolf Shall Dwell with the Lamb.* St. Louis, MO: Chalice, 1993.

La Sor, William Sanford, David Allan Hubbard, William Frederick Bush, James R. Battenfield, Robert L. Hubbard, Jr., and William B. Nelson, Jr. *Old Testament Survey: The Message, Form, and Background of the Old Testament.* 2d. ed. Grand Rapids: Eerdmans, 1996.

Lea, Thomas D. and Hayne P. Griffin, Jr. *The New American Commentary: 1, 2 Timothy & Titus.* Vol. 34. Nashville: Broadman, 1992.

Lencioni, Patrick. *The Five Dysfunctions of a Team.* San Francisco: Jossey-Bass, 2002.

Little, Helen. *Volunteers: How to Get Them and How to Keep Them.* Naperville, IL: Panacea, 1999.

Longenecker, Richard N. *The Ministry and Message of Paul.* Grand Rapids: Zondervan, 1971.

Maddox Robert L., Jr. *Layman's Bible Book Commentary: Acts.* Vol. 19. Nashville: Broadman: 1979.

Malphurs, Aubrey. *Values-Driven Leadership: Discovering and Developing Your Core Values for Ministry.* Grand Rapids: Baker, 1996.

Maldonado Pérez Zaida. "U.S. Hispanic/ Latino Identity and Protestant Experience: A Brief Introduction for the Seminarian." *Hispanic Theological Initiave, Perspectivas: Occasional Papers.* (Fall 2003): 93-110.

Mancari, Joseph Wayne. "Equipping Disciples: A Training Program for Identifying, Recruiting, Mentoring and Releasing Lay Leaders." D.Min. diss., Regent University, 2002.

McGee, J. Vernon. *Thru The Bible. I Corinthians Through Revelation.* Vol. v. Nashville: Thomas Nelson, 1983

McLaren, Brian. The Church on the Other Side. Grand Rapids: Eerdmans, 2000.

McClung, Grant. *Globalbeliever.com: Connecting to God's Work in your World.* Cleveland, TN: Pathway Press, 2000.

Mejido, Manuel J. "U. S. Hispanics/ Latinos and the Field of Graduate Theological Education," *Theological Education* 34: no. 2 (1998): 59-71.

Meltzer, Milton. *The Hispanic Americans.* New York: Thomas Y. Crowell, 1982.

Miller, Darrow L. *Discipling Nations: The Power of Truth to Transform Cultures.* Seattle, WA: YWAM Publishing, 2001.

Montoya, Alex. *Hispanic Ministry in North America.* Grand Rapids: Zondervan, 1987.

Moore, Joan and Harry Pachon. *Hispanics in the United States.* Englewood Cliffs, NJ: Prentice-Hall. 1985.

Morales, Ed. Living in Spanglish. New York: St. Martin's Press, 2002.

Murray, Andrew. *The Key to the Missionary Problem.* Fort Washington, PA: CLC Publications, 2001.

Myers, Bryant L. Exploring World Mission. Monrovia, CA: World Vision, 2003.

Neuhaus, Richard John, ed. *Theological Education and Moral Formation.* Grand Rapids: Eerdmans, 1992.

Newton, Taer R, and Kjell Erik Rudestam. *Your Statistical Consultant: Answers to Your Data Analysis Questions.* Thousand Oaks, CA: Sage Publications, 1999.

Niemi, John A. and Dennis D. Gooler. Technologies for Learning Outside the Classroom. *New Directions for Continuing Education.* San Francisco: Jossey-Bass, 1987.

Nouwen, Henri. *In the Name of Jesus: Reflections on Christian Leadership.* New York: Crossroad, 1998.

Núñez, Emilio A. *Hacia una Misionología Evangélica Latinoamericana.* Miami: Editorial Unilit, 1997.

Ortiz, Manuel. *One New People: Models for Developing Multiethnic Church.* Downers Grove: InterVarsity, 1996.

Oshry, Barry. *Seeing Systems: Unlocking the Mysteries of Organizational Life.* San Francisco: Berrett-Koehler, 1995.

Pacala, Leon. *The Role of ATS in Theological Education 1980-1990.* Atlanta: Scholars Press, 1998.

Padilla, C. René. *Bases Bíblicas de la Misión: Perspectivas Latinoamericanas.* Buenos Aires, Argentina: William B. Eerdmans, 1998.

_____. *De la Marginación al Compromiso.* Florida: Buenos Aires-Argentina: Fraternidad Teológica Latinoamericana, 1991.

_____. *De la Marginación al Compromiso.* Florida: Buenos Aires- Argentina: Fraternidad Teológica Latinoamericana, 1991.

Passing the Torch: Leadership: 14 Studies on 1 & 2 Timothy, 2d ed. Littleton, CO: Serendipity House, 1998.

Payton, Melissa. *The Prentice Hall Guide to Evaluating Online Resources with research Navigator.* Upper Saddle River, NJ: Pearson Education, 2004.

Pedraja, Luis G. *Teología: An Introduction to Hispanic Theology.* Nashville: Abingdon, 2003.

Perraton, Hilary and Helen Lentell. *Policy for Open and Distance Learning.* New York: RoutledgeFalmer, 2004.

Petersen, Douglas. No con Ejército, ni con Fuerza. Miami, FL: Editorial Vida, 1998.

Peterson, Eugene H. *Working the Angles: The Shape of Pastoral Integrity.* Grand Rapids: Eerdmans, 1987.

Pfeiffer, Markus L. "Christian Vision and Destiny: a Seminar Workbook and Christian Leader Guide to Developing a Life Vision Statement." D.Min. diss., Regent University, 2003.

Pine, B. Joseph, II, and James H. Gilmore. *The Experience Economy: Work is Theatre & Every Business a Stage.* Boston: Harvard Business School Press, 1999.

Porter, Stanley E. Paul in Acts. Peabody, MA: Hendrickson, 2001.

Ramírez, David E. *Educación Teológica y Misión hacia el Siglo XXI.* Quito, Ecuador: FLEREC, 2002.

Ramirez, Roberto R. and G. Patricia de la Cruz. *The Hispanic Population in the United States: March 2002.* U.S. Census Bureau, Current Population Reports P20-545. Washington DC: GPO.

Ramsay, William M. *The Education of Christ.* New Canaan: CT, Keats Publishing, 1981.

Recinos, Harold J. *Jesus Weep: Global Encounters on Our Doorstep.* Nashville: Abingdon Press, 1992.

Rhodes, Stephen. *Where the Nations Meet: The Church in a Multicultural World.* Downers Grove: InterVarsity, 1998.

Rouch, Mark. *Competent Ministry: A Guide to Effective Continuing Education.* Nashville: Abingdon, 1974.

Rowntree, Derek. *Making Materials-Based Learning Work.* Sterling, VA: Kogan Page, 1997.

Sánchez, Daniel R. *Hispanic Realities Impacting America.* Ft. Worth, TX: Church Starting Network, 2007.

Sánchez, Daniel R. *Realidades Hispanas Que Impactan A América.* Ft. Worth, TX: Church Starting Network, 2008.

Schreiter, Robert J. "The ATS Globalization and Theological Education Project: Contextualization from a World Perspective." *Theological Education* 30, no. 2 (Spring 1994): 81-88.

Seifrid, Mark A. and Randall K. J. Tan. *The Pauline Writings: An Annotated Bibliography.* Grand Rapids: Baker, 2002.

Seifter, Harvey and Peter Economy. *Leadership Ensemble.* New York, NY: Times Books, 2001.

Simons, George F., Carmen Vasquez, and Philip R. Harris. *Transcultural Leadership.* Houston: Gulf Publishing Company, 1993.

Silva, Kenneth Joseph. "An Explosion of Evangelism in your Church: Introducing the 'Share Your Faith Workshop.'" D.Min. diss., Regent University, 2002.

Simpson, Ormond. *Supporting Students in Open and Distance Learning.* Sterling, VA: Kogan Page Limited, 2000.

Sincich, Terry, David M. Levine, and David Stephan. *Practical Statistics by Example Using Microsoft Excel and Minitab,* 2d ed. Upper Saddle River, NJ: Prentice Hall, 2002.

Slotki, I. W. *Kings, Hebrew Text & English Translation with an Introduction and Commentary.* London: The Soncino Press, 1966.

Spohn, William C. *Go and Do Likewise: Jesus and Ethics.* New York: Continuum, 1999.

Snook, Stewart G. *Developing Leaders Through Theological Education by Extension* Wheaton, IL: Billy Graham Center, 1992.

Solivan, Samuel. *The Spirit, Pathos and Liberation.* Sheffield: England. Sheffield Academic Press, 1998.

Stackhouse, Max L. "Contextualization and Theological Education." *Theological Education* 23, no. 1 (1986): 67-84.

_____. *Apologia: Contextualization, Globalization, and Mission in Theological Education.* Grand Rapids: Eerdmans, 1988.

Stanton, Graham N. *The Gospels and Jesus.* New York: Oxford University Press, 1989.

Stier, Rudolf. *Words of the Apostles.* Minneapolis: Klock & Klock, 1981.

Streifer, Philip A. *Using Data to Make Better Educational Decisions.* Lanham, MD: Scarecrow Press, 2002.

Suárez, Marcelo M. and Mariela M. Páez. *Latinos Remaking America.* Los Angeles: University of California Press, 2002.

Suro, Roberto. *Strangers Among US: Latinos Lives in a Changing America.* New York: Vintage Books, 1999.

Taylor, William David. *Internationalizing Missionary Training: A Global Perspective.* Grand Rapids, MI: Baker, 1992.

Terry, Robert. *Seven Zones for Leadership.* Palo Alto, CA: Davies-Black Publishing, 2001.

Terwel, Jan and Decker Walker. *Curriculum as Shaping Force: Toward a Principled Approach in Curriculum Theory and Practice.* New York: Nova Science, 2004.

2000-2001 Fact Book on Theological Education (Pittsburgh: The Association of Theological Schools).

Turabian, Kate L. *A Manual for Writers of Terms Papers, Theses, and Dissertations* 6th ed. Chicago: University of Chicago Press, 1996.

Umidi, Joseph. *Confirming the Pastoral Call.* Grand Rapids: Kregel, 2000.

Urrabazo, Rosendo. "Pastoral education of Hispanic Adults," *Missiology* 20 no. 2 (2001): 255-260.

U.S. Census Bureau. *The Hispanic Population in the United States: March 2002, Current Population Reports, P20-545.* Washington, D.C.: GPO, 2002.

U.S. Bureau of the Census. *Census of Population & Housing.* Washington, D.C.: GPO, 2000.

Van Gelder, Craig, ed. Confident Witness-Changing World. Grand Rapids: Eerdmans Publishing Co., 1999.

Vandervert, Larry R, Larisa V. Shavinina, and Richard A. Cornell. *Cyber Education: The Future of Long Distance Learning.* Larchmont, NY: Mary Ann Liebert, 2001.

Villafañe, Eldin. *The Liberating Spirit Berating Spirit: Toward an Hispanic American Pentecostal Social Ethic.* Grand Rapids: William B. Eerdmans, 1993.

Villafañe, Eldin, Bruce W. Jackson, Robert A. Evans, and Alice Frazer Evans. *Transforming the City: Reframing Education for Urban Ministry.* Grand Rapids: William B. Eerdmans, 2002.

Ward, Ronald A. Commentary on 1 & 2 Timothy & Titus. Waco, TX: Word Books, 1974.

Wagner, C. Peter. The New Apostolic Churches. Ventura: Gospel Light, 1998.

Weiss, Juanita. Interview by author, 18 January 2005, Virginia Beach, VA,.

Westcott, Brooke Foss. St. *Paul's Epistle to the Ephesians.* Grand Rapids: Eerdmans, 1950.

Whang, Henry Kyuil. "A New Model for Theological Education in Korean Church *Context: Centered on the Curriculum for Minor Schools.*" Ph. D. diss., Regent University, 1999.

Wheeler, Barbara G. "The Faculty members of the Future: How Are They Being Shaped." *The Christian Century* 115, no. 4 (F 4-11 1998): 106-109; 111.

Whitehead, James D. and Evelyn Eaton Whitehead. *Method in Ministry: Theological Reflection and Christian Ministry.* Kansas City, MO: Sheed & Ward, 1995.

Wiater, Diane Marie. "Transformational Leadership: An Examination of Significant Leadership Development Life Experiences of Selected Doctor of Ministry Students." Ph.D. diss., Regent University, 2001.

Williams, J. Rodman. *Renewal Theology*. Grand Rapids: Zondervan, 1996.

Wiseman, Donald J. *Tyndale Old Testament Commentaries. 1 & 2 Kings, An Introduction & Commentary.* Downers Grove, IL: Inter-Varsity, 1993.

Wood, Charles, M. "Theological Inquiry and Theological Education." *Theological Education* XXI, no. 2 (1985): 73-93.

APPENDICES

APPENDIX 1
TIDEWATER DEMOGRAPHIC RESEARCH

Because of my desire for training Hispanic pastors and leaders for ministry, I spent the last seven years working with almost every Hispanic church in the Tidewater area. The Lord put in my heart to gather basic information about these churches. Thus, I began to interview Hispanic leaders to gather this data.

I collected church addresses, phone numbers, the pastors' and church email addresses, and the number of people who worship in each church. Additionally, I assembled the times of worship services. I entered this information into a database.

Many ministers, pastors, and laypersons have contacted me to obtain information for outreach to the Hispanic community or further research about the region's Hispanic population. I maintain the database on my computer and update it when I learn of new Hispanic churches that are formed in the Tidewater area.

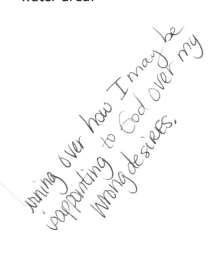

APPENDIX 2
REGENT HISPANIC ENROLLMENT

Regent Data	SP04	FALL 04	SP05	FALL 05
Total Students	3220	3173	3675	2490
Divinity Students	568	563	620	485
Total Hispanic Students	93	111	107	95
Total Hispanics Divinity	13	20	18	12
Percentage Hispanics in School	2.9	3.5	2.9	3.8
Percentage Hispanics in Divinity School	2.2	3.6	2.9	2.5

Wow! Most people Hispanic or otherwise do not see degrees in Divinity ao being lucrative. Could this be a reason why there may not ao many ao would like to see. Do people feel they can earn a living God's? this population?

APPENDIX 3-A
SURVEY TO THE HISPANIC PASTORS
AND LEADERS

The following survey has been elaborated for the purpose of evaluating the level of education of the leaders and pastors in the state of Virginia. I want to thank you for the time you will invest answering sincerely this questionnaire. It is not necessary to write your name and the information is confidential.

I. General Information

(Please mark with an "X" and complete the questions)

Pastor _____ Leader _____ Years in the ministry _____
Marital status: Single _____ Married: _____ Age: _____
Place of birth: City _____ Country _____
Denomination/Church: _____
Resident? _____ Citizen? _____ N/A _____

II. Level of Education

Highest Level of education that you have attained:

a) Elementary _____ b) High School _____ c) Associate Degree _____
d) College Degree _____ e) Master Degree _____ f) Doctorate _____
Years of study:

a) Elementary _____ b) High School _____ c) Associate Degree _____
d) College Degree _____ e) Masters Degree _____ f) Doctorate _____
Titles obtained, name of the institution, and place:

Title	Institution	Place

III. Computer Competency

Do you have a computer at home? Yes _____ No _____

How do you consider your knowledge in computers?

Poor _____ Basic _____ Intermediate _____ Advanced _____

141

Do you have access to the Internet?   Yes _____

Do you have computer at work?   Yes _____ No _____

IV. Preferences of Study

In what model of theological program would you be interested?

a) Non-formal (not Academic) _____ b) Formal (Academic) _____
If you had the opportunity to advance your studies of theological
   education, what would be the maximum level that you would
   like to achieve?

a) Certificate _____ b) Diploma _____ c) High School Diploma _____
d) Master Degree _____ e) Doctoral _____
What would be your preference?

a) On campus _____ b) By Internet _____ c) Distance Education _____
d) Mentoring _____ e) Combination of _____ and _____
If your choice is on campus, what would be your preference?

a) 1-3 times during the week _____ b) Saturdays (AM/PM) _____
c) During weekends (Friday night and Saturday morning) _____
d) One intensive week by class (modular)_____
e) An intensive weekend per class_____
f) Mentoring _____

142

What is the biggest obstacle for getting more training? Enumerate from 1-5 in order of preference, where 1 is most important and 5 is least important for you.

a) Finances _____ b) Time _____ c) Ministry Responsibilities _____
d) Lack of the English language _____
e) Lack of adequate programs _____

What much time are you willing to travel to study?

a) Less than one hour _____ b) more than one hour _____
c) I am not willing to travel _____

What would it be your greater motivation to attain theological training? Enumerate from 1-5 in order of preference, where 1 is most important and 5 is least important for you.

a) Greater knowledge of the Word of God (   )
b) To serve in the church in some ministry (   )
c) To improve my life devotional (   )
d) To discover my spiritual gifts (   )
e) To learn to study the Bible (   )
f) I recognize the importance to get more training (   )
g) To plant a new church (   )
h) To respond adequately to God's call (   )
i) To be part of a ministry team (   )

What would be the area of study of greatest interest for you? Enumerate from 1-5 in order of preference, where 1 is most important and 5 is least important for you.

a) Pastoring _____ b) Evangelism _____ c) Teaching _____
d) Discipleship _____ e) Church Planting _____ f) Counseling _____
g) Leadership _____ h) Christian Education _____ i) Missions _____
j) Social Service _____ k) Arts/Communications _____
l) Administration _____

How would you finance your studies?

a) Personal Savings _____ b) Scholarship c) Bank Loan _____
d) financial Support from churches _____ e) Another method _____

Additional Comments:

_____
_____
_____

_____   _____

_____

_____

_____

_____

_____

_____

_____

_____

_____

APPENDIX 3-B
SURVEY IN SPANISH

Encuesta para Pastores y Líderes Hispanos en Virginia
Programa Piloto

La siguiente encuesta ha sido elaborada con el propósito de evaluar el nivel de educación de los líderes y pastores en el estado de Virginia. Gracias por el tiempo que usted invertirá contestando sinceramente este cuestionario. No es necesario escribir su nombre y la información es confidencial.

I. Información General

(Favor de marcar con una "X" y llenar los espacios correspondientes)

Pastor _____ Líder_____ Años en el ministerio _____
Estado Civil: Soltero _____ Casado: _____ Edad: _____
Lugar de nacimiento: Ciudad _____, País _____
Denominación/ iglesia: _____
Residente _____ Ciudadano _____, N/A _____

II. Nivel de educación General

1) Nivel más alto de educación que usted ha alcanzado:

a) Primaria _____ b) Bachillerato/Técnico _____ c) Tecnológico _____
d) Licenciatura _____ e) Maestría _____ f) Doctorado _____
Años de estudio:

a) Primaria _____ b) Bachillerato _____ c) Licenciatura _____
d) Maestría _____ e) Doctorado _____

Títulos obtenidos, nombre de la institución y lugar:

_____

_____

III. Manejo/ conocimiento del Computador

¿Tiene usted computador en casa?   Si _____ No _____

¿Cómo considera usted el manejo y conocimiento del computador?

Pobre _____ Básico _____ Intermedio _____ Avanzado _____
¿Tiene usted acceso al Internet?   Si _____ No _____

¿Tiene usted computador en su trabajo?   Si _____ No _____

IV. Preferencias de Estudio

¿En qué clase de programa teológico estaría usted interesado?

a) Informal (No académico) _____ b) Formal (Académico) _____
Su usted tuviera la oportunidad de avanzar sus estudios de
educación teológica, ¿Cuál sería el nivel máximo que le
gustaría alcanzar?

a) Certificado _____ b) Diploma _____ c) Bachillerato _____
d) Maestría _____ e) Doctorado _____
¿Cuál sería su preferencia?

a) Presencial _____ b) Por Internet _____ c) A Distancia _____
d) Mentoría _____ e) Combinación de _____ y _____
Si fuera presencial, ¿cuál sería su preferencia?

a) 1-3 veces Durante la semana _____ b) Sábados (AM/PM) _____
c) Durante los fines de semana (viernes en la noche y sábado en la
mañana) _____ d) 1 semana intensiva por clase (modular) _____
e) Un fin de semana intensivo por material _____ f) Mentoría
personalizada _____
¿Cuál considera usted que es el obstáculo más grande para que la
gente se prepare? (Del 1 al 5 enumere los siguientes, siendo 1
el más importante y 5 el de menor importancia)

a) Finanzas _____ b) Tiempo _____ c) Ministerio _____ d) Carencia
del idioma Inglés _____ e) Carencia de programas adecuados _____
¿Qué distancia estaría usted dispuesto a viajar para estudiar?

a) Menos de una hora _____ b) Más de una hora _____
c) No estoy dispuesto a viajar _____

¿Cuál sería su mayor motivación para seguir preparándose teológicamente? Enumere de 1-5 en orden de preferencia, siendo 1 el más importante y 5 el menos importante para usted.

a) Mayor conocimiento de la Palabra de Dios (   )
b) Servir en la iglesia en algún ministerio (   )
c) Mejorar mi vida devocional (   )
d) Descubrir mis dones espirituales (   )
e) Aprender a estudiar la Biblia (   )
f) Reconozco la importancia de prepararme mejor (   )
g) Plantar una nueva iglesia (   )
h) Responder adecuadamente al llamado de Dios (   )
i) Ser parte de un equipo ministerial (   )

¿Cual sería el área de estudio de mayor interés para usted? Enumere de 1-5 en orden de preferencia, siendo 1 el más importante y 5 el menos importante para usted.

a) Pastorado _____ b) Evangelismo _____ c) Enseñanza _____
d) Discipulado _____ e) Plantación de iglesias _____
f) Consejería _____ g) Liderazgo _____ h) Educación Cristiana _____
i) Misiones _____ j) Servicio Social _____
k) Arte/Comunicaciones _____ l) Administración _____
¿Cómo financiaría sus estudios?

a) Ahorros personales _____ b) Obtención de beca _____
c) Préstamo bancario _____ d) Apoyo financiero de la iglesia _____
e) Otro método _____
Comentarios y/o inquietudes adicionales:

_____
_____
_____
_____
_____
_____
_____
_____
_____
_____

APPENDIX 4-A

HISPANIC PASTORS AND LEADERS
COUNTRY

Country	Number	Percent
Colombia	9	29
El Salvador	7	23
Venezuela	6	19
Bolivia	3	10
México	3	10
Guatemala	2	6
Chile	1	3
Total	31	100

APPENDIX 4-B

HISPANIC PASTORS AND LEADERS
MARITAL STATUS

Marital Status	Number	Percent
Married	16	52
Single	13	42
Widowed	2	6
Total	31	100

APPENDIX 4-C

HISPANIC PASTORS
AND LEADERS; GENDER

Gender	Number
Male	16
Female	15
Total	**31**

APPENDIX 4-D

PASTORS AND LEADERS;
DENOMINATIONAL BACKGROUND

Denomination	Number	Percent
Independent	22	72
Church of God	6	19
Ekklesia	2	6
Baptist	1	3
Total	31	**100**

APPENDIX 4-E

HISPANIC PASTORS AND
LEADERS; LEVEL OF EDUCATION

Level of Education	Number	Percent
Elementary Completion	4	1
Up to 8th Grade	1	3
9th-11th Grade	2	6
High School Completion	19	62
Community College	1	3
Master's Degree	3	10
Doctorate Degree	1	3

APPENDIX 4-F

HISPANIC PASTORS AND
LEADERS; PEOPLE'S PREFERENCES

Response	Number	Percent
Yes	14	45
Not	4	13
Uncertain	9	29
Not Response	4	13
Total	**31**	**100**

APPENDIX 4-G

HISPANIC PASTORS
AND LEADERS; MOTIVATIONS

Motivation to Attain Theological Training		
1. To know more about the Bible		
2. To improve the study of the Bible		
3. To serve in the local church		
4. To identify the Spiritual Gifts		
5. To improve devotional life		
Highest Level of Education That You Want to Attain		
Level of Education	Number	Percent
High School Completion	1	3
Certificate	1	3
Diploma	6	19
Master Degree	6	19
Doctorate Program	17	56
Total	31	100

APPENDIX 4-H

HISPANIC PASTORS AND LEADERS; GENERAL INFORMATION

Number of Years of Experience in the Ministry
16 people answered this question
15 people did not answer
Average 103.5/16 = 6.5 Years

Average Age of the People
22 people did answer
9 people did not answer
Numbers: 888/22 = 40.36
Median: 40.4 Years
Oldest person: 57 Years
Youngest person: 26 Years

Denominational Background
Independent Churches: 22
Church of God: 6
Ekklesia USA: 2
Baptist: 1
5 churches represented

Major Obstacles of the People to Study
1. Finances
2. Lack of Time (limitations)
3. Lack of English Proficiency
4. Full Time Ministry
5. Inadequate Programs of study

Favorite Fields of Study
1.Teaching and doctrine
2. Leadership
3. Counseling
4. Christian Education
5. Evangelism
6. Discipleship

APPENDIX 5 A

A LEADERSHIP CERTIFICATE
APPLICATION FORM

Full Name

_____

(Last)   (First)   (Middle)

Semester desiring to begin program: ___Spring ___Fall Year: 200___

Address:

_____

City: _____State:_____
Zip:_____

Phone:_____ _____
_____
         (Home)   (Work)
                (Mobile)

Church/ Name: _____ Your
Position:_____

Denomination/Affiliation:_____ E-mail:_____

Pastor's Name: _____ Phone:
_____

Marital Status:. ___Single ___Married Maiden
Name:_____

Gender: ____Male ____Female   Age: _____Years

Country of Origin: _____
         Birthdate:_____

(Month/day/year)

Years living in USA: _____ Years   Are you fluent in
English: ____Yes ___Not

153

COMPUTER COMPETENCY	YES	NO
Do you have access to the Internet?		
Do you know how to use a computer?		
Do you know how to surf in the Internet?		
Do you have an e-mail account?		
Do you know how to send and receive emails?		

ENGLISH PROFICIENCY	HIGH	BASIC	LOW
How is your level of spoken English?			
How is your level of written English?			

LEVEL OF EDUCATION

High School/College	Major	Degree/credits	GPA	Dates Attended

References: List the name/contact information of the requested references. HLCP'S staff may contact these references as a standard part of the admissions qualification process. Please inform references of this possibility.

References	Name & Title	Relation ship	Years Known	Phones
Pastor				
Leader/ Friend				
Mentor				

CONTRACT OF PERSONAL COMMITMENT WITH THE HISPANIC LEADERSHIP CERTIFICATE PROGRAM

I, _____, in front of God and of my brothers, I compromise to initiate and to finish the program "Hispanic Leadership Certificate" complying with the tasks and assignments of each matter, assuming my financial obligations in time and form stipulated, trusting in the strength of the Lord to finish with excellence this program.

My Covenantal Scripture:

_____

Signature: _____

Date:_____

This ministered to me about my current education.

APPENDIX 5-B

APPLICATION FORM TRANSLATED
IN SPANISH

Aplicación Certificado en Liderazgo Hispano
Nombre completo

_____
               (Apellido)   (Primer Nombre)
    (Segundo nombre)

Semestre de inicio: ___Primavera___Otoño Año: 200___

Dirección:_____

Ciudad: _____Estado:_____ Código

Postal:_____

Teléfono:_____ _____
         (Casa)   (Trabajo)

Nombre de la Iglesia: _____
Posición:_____

Denominación:_____
Correo@:_____

Nombre del Pastor: _____ Teléfono:
_____

Estado Civil. ___Soltero ___Casado Divorciado___ Otro
Nombre:_____

Genero: ____Masculino ____Femenino   Edad:_____Años

País de Origen: _____

Fecha de Nacimiento: _____

(Mes/día/año)

Años en USA: _____ Años

MANEJO DE COMPUTADORAS	SI	NO
¿Tiene acceso a una computadora con conexión a Internet?		
¿Sabe utilizar una computadora?		
¿Sabe utilizar el Internet?		
¿Tiene correo electrónico?		
¿Sabe enviar y recibir correos electrónicos?		

CONOCIMIENTO DEL IDIOMA INGLÉS	ALTO	MEDIO	BAJO
¿Cómo está su nivel de inglés hablado?			
¿Cómo está su nivel de inglés escrito?			

Colegio/ Universidad	Clase/ tipo	Diploma/ Créditos	Promedio de Calificaciones	Fechas

NIVEL DE EDUCACIÓN

Referencias: Enumere y complete la siguiente información. Parte del proceso de admisión incluye la verificación de referencias personales.

Referencias	Nombre & Titulo	Relación	Años de conocido	Teléfonos
Pastor				
Líder/ amigo				
Mentor				

159

CONTRATO DE COMPROMISO PERSONAL CON EL PROGRAMA CERTIFICADO EN LIDERAZGO HISPANO

Yo, _____, delante de Dios y de mis hermanos, me comprometo a iniciar y a terminar el programa "Certificado en Liderazgo Hispano" cumpliendo con las tareas y asignaciones de cada materia, asumiendo mis obligaciones financieras en tiempo y forma estipuladas, confiando en la fortaleza del Señor para terminar con excelencia este programa.

Mi Versículo de pacto es: _____

Firma: _____

Fecha:_____

APPENDIX 5-C

STUDENTS' PROFILE,
MINISTRY INVOLVEMENT

	Number
Pastor	3
Pastor's Wife	2
Serving in Church	13
Not Yet Serving	4
Total	22

APPENDIX 6-A

HLCP STUDENT ENTRANCE PROFILE

Marital Status: Single _____ Married _____ Divorced _____
                 Widowed _____
Gender: Male _____ Female _____   Age: _____ Years
Country of Origin: _____
Serves in the church: YES _____ NO _____
*This program of Hispanic leadership has been designed to facilitate the spiritual growth focused in the profile of the leadership. 4 areas in the following questionnaire have been selected. Respond the following (17) questions marking with an "X" the answer that you consider more adequate.

CHARACTERISTIC #1

1)   The model of leadership of Jesus is not clear.

   a) Strongly Disagree _____ (b) Disagree _____ (c) Not sure _____
   d) Agree _____ e) Strongly Agree _____

   Jesus found solutions to the problems of the people.

   a) Strongly Disagree _____ (b) Disagree _____ (c) Not sure _____
   d) Agree _____ e) Strongly Agree _____

   The conviction of Jesus for the things that he did was weak.

   a) Strongly Disagree _____ (b) Disagree _____ (c) Not sure _____
   d) Agree _____ e) Strongly Agree _____

   I am imitating the model of leadership of Jesus in my life.

   a) Strongly Disagree _____ (b) Disagree _____ (c) Not sure _____
   d) Agree _____ e) Strongly Agree _____

CHARACTERISTIC #2

1)   Jesus did not pay a lot of attention to the lack of character of the people that he ministered.

a) Strongly Disagree _____ (b) Disagree _____ (c) Not sure _____
d) Agree _____ e) Strongly Agree _____

The model of leadership of Jesus helps me to identify the weaknesses and strengthens in my personal life.

a) Strongly Disagree _____ (b) Disagree _____ (c) Not sure _____
d) Agree _____ e) Strongly Agree _____

The meditation in the Word of God has not helped me to identify the weaknesses of my character.

a) Strongly Disagree _____ (b) Disagree _____ (c) Not sure _____
d) Agree _____ e) Strongly Agree _____

The Christian leader does not need to evaluate constantly his spiritual condition.

a) Strongly Disagree _____ (b) Disagree _____ (c) Not sure _____
d) Agree _____ e) Strongly Agree _____

CHARACTERISTIC #3
1) Prayer is not very important in the life of a leader.

a) Strongly Disagree _____ (b) Disagree _____ (c) Not sure _____
d) Agree _____ e) Strongly Agree _____

The leader should depend on God in some areas of his life.

a) Strongly Disagree _____ (b) Disagree _____ (c) Not sure _____
d) Agree _____ e) Strongly Agree _____

The leader goes first to God with the problem.

a) Strongly Disagree _____ (b) Disagree _____ (c) Not sure _____
d) Agree _____ e) Strongly Agree _____

The ministry of the Holy Spirit is not so important to receive God's guidance.

a) Strongly Disagree _____ (b) Disagree _____ (c) Not sure _____
d) Agree _____ e) Strongly Agree _____

CHARACTERISTIC #4   Not sure I understand the question.

1)   You have been planned to please God.

a) Strongly Disagree _____ (b) Disagree _____ (c) Not sure _____
d) Agree _____ e) Strongly Agree _____

You have been created to be isolated from God's family.

a) Strongly Disagree _____ (b) Disagree _____ (c) Not sure _____
d) Agree _____ e) Strongly Agree _____

You have been created by God to serve God and others.

a) Strongly Disagree _____ (b) Disagree _____ (c) Not sure _____
d) Agree _____ e) Strongly Ag 162 _

You have been created by God without a specific purpose.

a) Strongly Disagree _____ (b) Disagree _____ (c) Not sure _____
d) Agree _____ e) Strongly Agree _____

The leader should ignore the problems that he has in front

a) Strongly Disagree _____ (b) Disagree _____ (c) Not sure _____
d) Agree _____ e) Strongly Agree _____

APPENDIX 6-B

HLCP STUDENT ENTRANCE
PROFILE IN SPANISH

Nombre Completo: _____

Fecha: _____

    Estado Civil. _____Soltero(a) ___Casado(a)
_____Divorciado(a) ___ Viudo(a) _____

Genero: ____Masculino ____Femenino
    Edad:_____Años

País de Origen: _____   Sirve en la
iglesia: ___SI ____NO

*Este programa en liderazgo Hispano esta diseñado para facilitar el crecimiento espiritual enfocado en el perfil del liderazgo. Se han seleccionado 4 características en el siguiente cuestionario. Responda las siguientes (17) preguntas marcando con una "X" la respuesta que usted considere más adecuada.

CARACTERISTICA #1

1)   El modelo de liderazgo de Jesús no es claro.

    a) Desacuerda Firmemente _____ (b) Desacuerda _____
    c) neutral _____ (d) Acuerda _____
    e) Acuerda Firmemente _____
Jesús encontraba soluciones a los problemas de la gente.

    a) Desacuerda Firmemente _____ (b) Desacuerda _____
    c) neutral _____ (d) Acuerda _____
    e) Acuerda Firmemente _____
La convicción de Jesús por las cosas que hacia fue débil.

    a) Desacuerda Firmemente _____ (b) Desacuerda _____
    c) neutral _____ (d) Acuerda _____
    e) Acuerda Firmemente _____
Estoy imitando el modelo de liderazgo de Jesús en mi vida.

    a) Desacuerda Firmemente _____ (b) Desacuerda _____
    c) neutral _____ (d) Acuerda _____
    e) Acuerda Firmemente _____

CARACTERISTICA #2

1) Jesús no presto mucha atención a la falta de carácter de la gente que ministraba.

a) Desacuerda Firmemente _____ (b) Desacuerda _____
c) neutral _____ (d) Acuerda _____
e) Acuerda Firmemente _____

El modelo de liderazgo de Jesús me ayuda a identificar las debilidades y fortalezas en mi vida personal.

a) Desacuerda Firmemente _____ (b) Desacuerda _____
c) neutral _____ (d) Acuerda _____
e) Acuerda Firmemente _____

La meditación en la Palabra de Dios no me ha ayudado a identificar las debilidades de mi carácter.

a) Desacuerda Firmemente _____ (b) Desacuerda _____
c) neutral _____ (d) Acuerda _____
e) Acuerda Firmemente _____

El líder cristiano no necesita evaluar constantemente su condición espiritual.

a) Desacuerda Firmemente _____ (b) Desacuerda _____
c) neutral _____ (d) Acuerda _____
e) Acuerda Firmemente _____

CARACTERISTICA #3

1) La oración no es muy importante en la vida de un líder.

a) Desacuerda Firmemente _____ (b) Desacuerda _____
c) neutral _____ (d) Acuerda _____
e) Acuerda Firmemente _____

El líder debe depender de Dios en algunas áreas de su vida.

a) Desacuerda Firmemente _____ (b) Desacuerda _____
c) neutral _____ (d) Acuerda _____
e) Acuerda Firmemente _____

El líder va primero a Dios con el problema.

a) Desacuerda Firmemente _____ (b) Desacuerda _____
c) neutral _____ (d) Acuerda _____
e) Acuerda Firmemente _____

El ministerio del Espíritu Santo no es tan importante para recibir la guía de Dios.

a) Desacuerda Firmemente _____ (b) Desacuerda _____
c) neutral _____ (d) Acuerda _____
e) Acuerda Firmemente _____

CARACTERISTICA #4

1) Fuiste planeado para agradar a Dios.

a) Desacuerda Firmemente _____ (b) Desacuerda _____
c) neutral _____ (d) Acuerda _____
e) Acuerda Firmemente _____

Fuiste hecho para estar aislado de la familia de Dios.

a) Desacuerda Firmemente _____ (b) Desacuerda _____
c) neutral _____ (d) Acuerda _____
e) Acuerda Firmemente _____

Fuiste formado para servir a Dios y a los demás.

a) Desacuerda Firmemente _____ (b) Desacuerda _____
c) neutral _____ (d) Acuerda _____
e) Acuerda Firmemente _____

Fuiste creado por Dios sin un propósito específico.

a) Desacuerda Firmemente _____ (b) Desacuerda _____
c) neutral _____ (d) Acuerda _____
e) Acuerda Firmemente _____

El líder debe de ignorar los problemas que se le presentan

a) Desacuerda Firmemente _____ (b) Desacuerda _____
c) neutral _____ (d) Acuerda _____
e) Acuerda Firmemente _____

APPENDIX 6-C

SAMPLE STUDENT DATA BEFORE
AND AFTER HLCP

Question Number	ST1 Data Before	ST1 Data After
1	5	5
2	5	5
3	5	5
4	4	4
5	5	5
6	5	5
7	5	5
8	5	5
9	1	5
10	5	5
11	5	5
12	5	5
13	5	5
14	5	5
15	5	5
16	5	5
	75	79
	16 Questions	
	22 Students	Range 16-80

APPENDIX 6-D

STATISTICAL RESULTS
BEFORE THE HLCP

Name	Data Before (X)	Xavrge	X-Xavrge	(X-Xavrge)²
ST1	75	73.36	1.6	2.7
ST2	74	73.36	0.6	0.4
ST3	78	73.36	4.6	21.5
ST4	76	73.36	2.6	7.0
ST5	77	73.36	3.6	13.2
ST6	76	73.36	2.6	7.0
ST7	76	73.36	2.6	7.0
ST8	74	73.36	0.6	0.4
ST9	78	73.36	4.6	21.5
ST10	74	73.36	0.6	0.4
ST11	77	73.36	3.6	13.2
ST12	68	73.36	-5.4	28.7
ST13	65	73.36	-8.4	69.9
ST14	61	73.36	-12.4	152.8
ST15	76	73.36	2.6	7.0
ST16	74	73.36	0.6	0.4
ST17	76	73.36	2.6	7.0
ST18	61	73.36	-12.4	152.8
ST19	80	73.36	6.7	44.1
ST20	71	73.36	-2.4	5.6
ST21	72	73.36	-1.4	1.8
ST22	75	73.36	1.6	2.7
			0.08	567.1

Xavrge=Mean	73.4	
N = 22	N-1=21	
Range	19	
Variance (S^2)=	27	
Standard Deviation (S)	5.2	
CV=S/Xavrge	0.07 or 7%	

APPENDIX 6 E

STATISTICAL RESULTS
AFTER THE HLCP

Name	Data After (X)	Xavrge	X-Xavrge	(X-Xavrge)^2
ST1	79	75.3	3.7	13.6
ST2	68	75.3	-7.3	53.4
ST3	79	75.3	3.7	13.6
ST4	79	75.3	3.7	13.6
ST5	78	75.3	2.7	7.2
ST6	76	75.3	0.7	0.5
ST7	75	75.3	-0.3	0.1
ST8	68	75.3	-7.3	53.4
ST9	70	75.3	-5.3	28.2
ST10	79	75.3	3.7	13.6
ST11	79	75.3	3.7	13.6
ST12	77	75.3	1.7	2.9
ST13	79	75.3	3.7	13.6
ST14	74	75.3	-1.3	1.7
ST15	76	75.3	0.7	0.5
ST16	74	75.3	-1.3	1.7
ST17	73	75.3	-2.3	5.3
ST18	65	75.3	-10.3	106.3
ST19	76	75.3	0.7	0.5
ST20	76	75.3	0.7	0.5
ST21	78	75.3	2.7	7.2
ST22	79	75.3	3.7	13.6
			0.2	364.8

Xavrge=Mean	75.31
N = 22	N-1 =2 1
Range	14
Variance (S^2) =	17.37
Standard Deviation (S)	4.17
	0.055 or
CV=S/Xavrge	5.5%

APPENDIX 7-A
ONLINE HLCP EVALUATION FOR LH101 & LH102

Please rate the following statements about class LH101 Biblical Principles of Leadership. Circle your answer for each question.

	Strongly Disagree	Disagree	Neutral	Agree	Strongly Agree
It helped me to understand better the biblical bases of my responsibility as a Christian leader.	1	2	3	4	5
It helped me to value better my religious leaders.	1	2	3	4	5
It helped me to improve my leadership abilities.	1	2	3	4	5
It helped me to grow spiritually.	1	2	3	4	5
It offered me sufficient practical elements to apply in my task as a leader.	1	2	3	4	5
It helped me to be a better leader.	1	2	3	4	5
It helped me to be a better Christian.	1	2	3	4	5
It increased my expectations in regard to my leaders.	1	2	3	4	5
It increased my expectations in regard to my own leadership.	1	2	3	4	5
It brought awareness of my weaknesses as a leader.	1	2	3	4	5
It brought awareness of my strengths as a leader.	1	2	3	4	5

APPENDIX 7-B

ONLINE HLCP EVALUATION SURVEY IN SPANISH

EVALUACION ANONIMA DE LOS ESTUDIANTES EN EL INTERNET CLASES LH101 Y 102

Basado en una escala de 1 – 5, por favor indique si acuerda o desacuerda con las siguientes oraciones, teniendo en cuenta que:

1) Desacuerda firmemente 2) Desacuerda 3) Neutral
4) Acuerda 5) Acuerda firmemente

a) La materia LH101 Principios Bíblicos de Liderazgo me ayudo a entender mejor las bases bíblicas de mi responsabilidad como líder cristiano.
1) Desacuerda firmemente 2) Desacuerda 3) Neutral
4) Acuerda 5) Acuerda firmemente

b) La materia LH101 Principios Bíblicos de Liderazgo me ayudo a valorar mejor a mis líderes religiosos.
1) Desacuerda firmemente 2) Desacuerda 3) Neutral
4) Acuerda 5) Acuerda firmemente

c) La materia LH101 Principios Bíblicos de Liderazgo me ayudo a mejorar mis habilidades de liderazgo.
1) Desacuerda firmemente 2) Desacuerda 3) Neutral
4) Acuerda 5) Acuerda firmemente

d) La materia LH101 Principios Bíblicos de Liderazgo me ayudo a crecer espiritualmente.
1) Desacuerda firmemente 2) Desacuerda 3) Neutral
4) Acuerda 5) Acuerda firmemente

e) La materia LH101 Principios Bíblicos de Liderazgo me brindo suficientes elementos prácticos para aplicar en mi tarea como líder.
1) Desacuerda firmemente 2) Desacuerda 3) Neutral
4) Acuerda 5) Acuerda firmemente

f) La materia LH101 Principios Bíblicos de Liderazgo hizo de mí un mejor líder.
1) Desacuerda firmemente 2) Desacuerda 3) Neutral
4) Acuerda 5) Acuerda firmemente

g) La materia LH101 Principios Bíblicos de Liderazgo hizo de mí un mejor cristiano.
    1) Desacuerda firmemente 2) Desacuerda 3) Neutral
    4) Acuerda 5) Acuerda firmemente

h) La materia LH101 Principios Bíblicos de Liderazgo aumento mis expectativas respecto a mis líderes.
    1) Desacuerda firmemente 2) Desacuerda 3) Neutral
    4) Acuerda 5) Acuerda firmemente

i) La materia LH101 Principios Bíblicos de Liderazgo aumento mis expectativas respecto a mi propio liderazgo.
    1) Desacuerda firmemente 2) Desacuerda 3) Neutral
    4) Acuerda 5) Acuerda firmemente

j) La materia LH101 Principios Bíblicos de Liderazgo me hizo consciente de mis debilidades como líder.
    1) Desacuerda firmemente 2) Desacuerda 3) Neutral
    4) Acuerda 5) Acuerda firmemente

k) La materia LH101 Principios Bíblicos de Liderazgo me hizo consciente de mis fortalezas como líder.
    1) Desacuerda firmemente 2) Desacuerda 3) Neutral
    4) Acuerda 5) Acuerda firmemente

APPENDIX 7-C

ONLINE EVALUATION
RESULTS OF THE HLCP

Online Survey Results for the Class LH101

Ques	1	2	3	4	5	6	7	8	9	10	11
S1	5	5	5	5	5	5	5	5	5	5	5
S2	5	5	5	5	5	5	5	5	5	5	5
S3	5	5	5	5	5	5	5	5	5	5	5
S4	5	5	5	5	5	5	5	5	5	5	5
S5	5	5	5	5	5	5	4	5	5	5	5
S6	5	4	5	5	5	5	5	5	5	4	5
S7	5	5	5	5	5	5	5	5	5	5	5
S8	5	5	5	5	5	5	5	5	5	5	5
S9	4	5	4	4	4	3	4	5	5	5	3
S10	5	5	5	5	5	5	5	5	5	5	4
S11	5	4	4	4	4	4	4	4	5	5	4
S12	5	5	5	4	5	4	4	5	5	4	4
S13	5	4	5	5	5	5	5	5	5	5	5

Online Survey Results for the Class LH102

APPENDIX 7-D:

STATISTICAL RESULTS
OF ONLINE EVALUATION FOR LH101

Results for the Class LH101

Ques	1	2	3	4	5	6	7	8	9
S1	5	5	5	5	5	5	5	5	5
S2	5	5	5	5	5	5	5	5	5
S3	5	5	5	5	5	5	5	5	5
S4	5	5	5	5	5	5	5	5	5
S5	5	5	5	5	5	5	4	5	5
S6	5	4	5	5	5	5	5	5	5
S7	5	5	5	5	5	5	5	5	5
S8	5	5	5	5	5	5	5	5	5
S9	4	5	4	4	4	3	4	5	5
S10	5	5	5	5	5	5	5	5	5
S11	5	4	4	4	4	4	4	4	5
S12	5	5	5	4	5	4	4	5	5
S13	5	4	5	5	5	5	5	5	5
Score Possible	65	65	65	65	65	65	65	65	65
Total Score	64	62	63	62	63	61	61	64	65
%	98.5	95.4	96.9	95.4	96.9	93.8	93.8	98.5	100.0
SUM	688								
Average/ Mean (X)	52.9								

APPENDIX 7-E
STATISTICAL RESULTS OF ONLINE
EVALUATION FOR LH102

Results for the Class LH102

Ques	1	2	3	4	5	6	7	8	9	10
S1	5	5	5	5	5	5	5	5	5	5
S2	5	5	5	5	5	5	5	5	5	5
S3	5	5	5	5	5	5	5	5	5	5
S4	5	5	5	5	5	5	5	5	5	5
S5	5	5	5	5	5	5	5	5	5	5
S6	5	5	5	5	5	4	5	5	5	5
S7	4	5	5	5	4	4	5	5	5	5
S8	5	5	5	5	5	5	5	5	5	5
S9	5	5	5	5	5	5	5	5	5	5
S10	4	5	3	4	4	3	4	4	4	4
S11	5	5	5	5	5	5	5	5	5	5
S12	5	4	5	4	5	5	4	4	5	5
S13	4	3	4	5	5	4	4	4	4	4
S14	5	5	5	5	5	5	5	5	5	5
Score Possible	70	70	70	70	70	70	70	70	70	70
Total Score Question	67	67	67	68	68	65	67	67	68	68
%	95.7	95.7	95.7	97.1	97.1	92.8	95.7	95.7	97.1	97.1
SUM	739									
Average / Mean (X)	52.8									
Median	55									
Total Score Possible	55									
Total SUM Possible	770									
% Total	95.97									

APPENDIX 7-F
TAILORED RESULTS OF ONLINE
EVALUATION FOR LH101

Question	Answer	Number Responding This Way	Percent
1	4	1	7.7
1	5	12	92.3
2	4	2	16.7
2	5	10	83.3
3	4	2	15.4%
3	5	11	84.6
4	4	3	23.1
4	5	10	76.9
5	4	2	15.4
5	5	11	84.6
6	3	1	7.7
6	4	2	15.4
6	5	10	76.9
7	4	3	25.0
7	5	9	75.0
8	4	1	7.7
8	5	12	92.3
9	5	13	100.
10	4	2	15.4
10	5	11	84.6
11	3	1	8.3
11	4	2	16.7
11	5	9	75.0

APPENDIX 7-G
TAILORED RESULTS OF ONLINE
EVALUATION FOR LH102

Question	Answer	Number Responding This Way	Percent
1	4	3	21.4
1	5	11	78.6
2	3	1	7.1
2	4	1	7.1
2	5	12	85.7
3	3	1	7.1
3	4	1	7.1
3	5	12	85.7
4	4	2	15.4
4	5	11	84.6
5	4	2	14.3
5	5	12	85.7
6	3	1	7.7
6	4	2	15.4
6	5	10	76.9
7	4	3	21.4
7	5	11	78.6
8	4	3	21.4
8	5	11	78.6
9	4	2	14.3
9	5	12	85.7
10	4	2	14.3
10	5	12	85.7
11	3	1	7.1
11	4	1	7.1
11	5	12	85.7

APPENDIX 8-A
LH101 SYLLABUS IN ENGLISH

Biblical Principles of Leadership
Spring 2005
March 12-April 8

Regent University

Hispanic Leadership Certificate Program (HLCP)

The Hispanic Leadership Program promotes and facilitates practical training for Hispanic leaders, pastors and missionaries who wants to impact God's world through the Gospel of Jesus Christ. (Ephesians 4:11-12). It is the intention of this program to promote and utilize relevant resources and materials to equip emerging leaders to better serve their communities where God has called them. The Leadership Certificate Program is a join effort with Regent University through the Center for Latin American Leadership.

Instructor for This Course

Dr. Victor H. Cuartas
E-mail: victcua@regent.edu

Description of Course

The course will provide general orientation to the leadership certificate, its process and expectations in non-formal theological education as well as specific orientation to the Leadership Certificate Program. The course will introduce the Biblical basis for leadership. Special attention is given to Jesus' example as a leader and the implications for today's ministry.

Purpose of Course LH101

The motivating principle behind the program's design and this course is this: transformative learning is more likely to be achieved when designed and facilitated with clear end results in view. The Leadership Certificate Program has been designed to equip pastors and leaders to impact their communities effectively. Character and relationship with God is paramount in this process. The *Student Profile* is the basis of every learning experience, textbook selection and course dialogues in Blackboard.

179

The purpose of this course is:

A) To identify the Biblical model of leadership by reflecting on Jesus' ministry.

B) To renew our way of exercising leadership by analyzing your weaknesses and strengths as emerging leader.

Prerequisites

Leadership Certificate Program participants only. (Cohort 2005A).

Key Aspects to Consider

➢ Looking at Jesus as a leader

➢ The issue of the heart

➢ Establishing priorities

➢ Understanding God's times

➢ Recognizing our limitations

Course Goals

To recognize the Biblical principles related to leadership based on Jesus model.

To describe and list the main Characteristics of Jesus as leader

To contrast the Biblical model of leadership with today's society

Course Competencies

The student who effectively completes this course should be able to:

Apply Biblical principles of leadership in his/her life and ministry

Recognize and follow Jesus' example of leadership

Differentiate the current trends of leadership

Identify the weaknesses areas in terms of leadership that need to be strengthened by the Holy Spirit.

General Program Competencies

1. Recognizes and Follows Jesus Example of Leadership

2. Understands God's Will and Call

3. Focuses on God's Mission in Ministry

4. Conducts life with balance

5. Recognizes both Strengths and Weaknesses

6. Walks along others in Accountability

7. Eager for Spiritual Renewal in Self & Others

Core Values

HLTC exists for the purpose of bringing together and encouraging both nonformal and formal educational institutions that hold and serve the following values:

1) Commitment to the training of ministry workers and emerging leaders for the local churches and ministries.

2) Commitment to the partnering with churches and ministries for facilitating training among leaders, pastors and missionaries.

3) Commitment to the mobilization of the body of believers for missions and evangelism.

4) Commitment to congregational-based governed and administered programs of study.

5) Commitment to the development of character and Christian ethics.

6) Commitment to a restoration-renewal focus in the spirit of Acts 3:19-25.

7) Commitment to Spirit-filled revival and body-life ministry.

8) Commitment to the fostering of passionate spirituality.

9) Commitment to the development of spiritual gifts to serve in the churches.

10) Commitment to covenantal integrity, due process and community life.

11) Commitment to the ideals of life stewardship.

12) Commitment to eschatology of victory that advances God's kingdom.

13) Commitment to unity, diversity, and uniqueness in the body of Christ.

14) Commitment to prepare the people of God for spiritual life and Biblical ministry to expand God's kingdom.

Tuition Expenses

The cost for every course will be $125
Total of 4 Courses $500
This price does not include books, photocopies, and travel expenses to attend to Saturday's In-Session on campus. These expenses will be covered by the student.

Textbook Resources

Students are encouraged to shop competitively. It is recommended to buy the books in advance so that you can be ready for every course. Be certain to purchase the correct version or edition of the text as outlined in the Course Syllabus. Some Hispanic Distributors are: Pan de Vida, Distribuidora Peniel, and Fuente de Vida.
The following online bookstores are often used by Regent students and may waive shipping fees:
Amazon.com (www.amazon.com)
Barnes and Noble (www.bn.com)
Christian Book Distributors (www.christianbook.com). Additional materials (e.g., articles, websites, etc.) may be found in the Course Material section of Blackboard.

On Campus Session

This program recognizes the importance of personal interaction and team working. That is why is so important to attend to the session on Regent Campus for every course. During that Saturday the professors will use different alternatives that will be considered such as panel discussions, power point presentations, audio-visuals, class room discussion, small group interaction and strategizing, case studies, guest speakers, etc. It is possible that this approach may change after the research has begun.

Course Schedule

Course	Activity	Date	# of Points
	Cohort's Registration On Campus Student Entrance Profile	March 2-6	2
Orientation & LH101	Cohorts' Orientation On-Campus Session Both Groups (2)	March 12	4
	Post-Session Dialogue in Bb 1st week Bb Dialogue	March 14-19	2
	2nd week Bb Dialogue	March 21-26	2
	3rd week Bb Dialogue	March 28-April 2	2
	Application & Paper	April 4-8	2

Blackboard Assignments

Date	Text	Questions
Post-Session Discussion in Blackboard		
March 14-19	Briner, Bob and Ray Pritchard. Jesús el Líder Modelo, Tomo I.	Bb Question/ Dialogue
March 21-26	Briner, Bob and Ray Pritchard. Jesús el Líder Modelo, Tomo II.	Bb Questions/ Dialogue:
March 28-April 2	Murdock, Mike. Secretos del Liderazgo de Jesús. General Application of the topic	Bb Questions/ Dialogue:

Study Suggestions

a) Begin with prayer that the Holy Spirit will guide your study. We encourage you to communicate your prayer requests to your prayer partners.

b) Follow the recommendations given to you during the orientation session to ensure that you meet the Computer Standards and can use Blackboard proficiently.

c) Familiarize yourself with your textbooks and follow the course schedule for each assignment.

Method of Evaluation:

1) The orientation session is mandatory = 4 Points

2) On-Campus Session = 8 points
   Attendance and participation during each on-Campus Session = 2 Points
   4 *On-Campus* Sessions = 8 points

3) Post-Session Dialogues in Bb = 12 points
   3 postings in Blackboard per course (with interactions) = 3 points, that is 1 point per dialog.
   12 dialogues (including interaction with the cohort) = 12 points

4) Student Profile = 6 points
   Student Entrance Profile = 2 points
   Mid-course Student Profile = 2 points
   Final course Student Profile = 2 points

5) Final Project (At the end of the program) = 5 points
   The required score to pass each course is 5.
   The required score to get the leadership certificate is 35
   Total score for the program: 35

Course Attendance

Due to the fact that on-campus sessions (including the orientation session) in the Hispanic Leadership Program are condensed to one Saturday format, it is required that students attend all sections of the class. Please plan to arrive on time and arrange your schedule to stay until the end of class. Early departure may disturb the course experience for all who are participating and may negatively affect the final course evaluation.

Student Requirements

1) To follow the professor's instructions in terms of the assignments and due dates.

2) To pray and select one mentor, pastor or leader that will walk with you in this process while you are pursuing the leadership certificate program at Regent University.

3) To contact and select at least three intercessors who are committed to pray for you during this process. We encourage you to lift in your prayers the cohort members, staff and faculty members of the program.

Overall Schedule of the HLCP

Course	Activity	Date	# of Points
	Cohort's Registration On Campus Student Entrance Profile	Feb 15-16	2
	Getting all the books and materials Student Entrance Profile	Feb. 21-25	
Orientation & LH101	Cohorts' Orientation On-Campus Session	March 12	4 2
	Preparation, questions, and Bb testing	March 14-19	
	Post-Session Dialogue in Bb 1st week Bb Dialogue	March 21-26	1
	2nd week Bb Dialogue	March 28-April 2	1
	3rd week Bb Dialogue & Application	April 4-9	1
	Preparation and readings Course 2	April 11-15	
LH102	On-Campus Session	April 16	2
	Post-Session Dialogue in Bb 1st week Bb Dialogue	April 18-23	1

186

Course	Activity	Date	# of Points
	2nd week Bb Dialogue	April 25-30	1
	3rd week Bb Dialogue & Application	May 2-7	1
	Preparation and readings Course 3	May 9-13	
LH103	On-Campus Session Mid-Course Student Profile	May 14	2 2
	Post-Session Dialogue in Bb 1st week Bb Dialogue	May 16-21	1
	2nd week Bb Dialogue	May 23-28	1
	3rd week Bb Dialogue & Application	May 30-June 4	1
	Preparation and readings Course 4	June 6-10	
LH104	On-Campus Session	June 11	2
	Post-Session Dialogue in Bb 1st week Bb Dialogue	June 13-18	1
	2nd week Bb Dialogue	June 20-25	1
	3rd Bb week Dialogue &	June 27-July 1	1

Survey
Working on Final Project

Course	Activity	Date	# of Points
Cohort's Commissioni ng and Celebration	Regent Campus Final Course Student Profile	July 5	2
	Turning in Final Project		5
	Clearance and grades	June 6-8	
	Cohort 2005 Commencement Ceremony	July 9	

Biblical Principles

Biblical Principles (KJV)

1Timothy 3:1-7 (Qualifications for ministry)

[1]This *is* a true saying, If a man desire the office of a bishop, he desireth a good work. [2]A bishop then must be blameless, the husband of one wife, vigilant, sober, of good behaviour, given to hospitality, apt to teach; [3]Not given to wine, no striker, not greedy of filthy lucre; but patient, not a brawler, not covetous; [4]One that ruleth well his own house, having his children in subjection with all gravity; [5](For if a man know not how to rule his own house, how shall he take care of the church of God?) [6]Not a novice, lest being lifted up with pride he fall into the condemnation of the devil. [7]Moreover he must have a good report of them which are without; lest he fall into reproach and the snare of the devil.

Titus 1: 6-9

[6]If any be blameless, the husband of one wife, having faithful children not accused of riot or unruly. [7]For a bishop must be blameless, as the steward of God; not selfwilled, not soon angry, not given to wine, no striker, not given to filthy lucre; [8]But a lover of hospitality, a lover of good men, sober, just, holy, temperate; [9]Holding fast the faithful word as he hath been taught, that he may

188

be able by sound doctrine both to exhort and to convince the gainsayers.

2 Timothy 2:24-25 (Character development)

24And the servant of the Lord must not strive; but be gentle unto all *men*, apt to teach, patient, 25In meekness instructing those that oppose themselves; if God peradventure will give them repentance to the acknowledging of the truth;

2 Timothy 3:16-17 (Biblical foundation)

16All scripture *is* given by inspiration of God, and *is* profitable for doctrine, for reproof, for correction, for instruction in righteousness: 17That the man of God may be perfect, throughly furnished unto all good works.

2 Timothy 4:11-16 (Caring about others)

11Only Luke is with me. Take Mark, and bring him with thee: for he is profitable to me for the ministry. 12And Tychicus have I sent to Ephesus. 13The cloke that I left at Troas with Carpus, when thou comest, bring *with thee*, and the books, *but* especially the parchments. 14Alexander the coppersmith did me much evil: the Lord reward him according to his works: 15Of whom be thou ware also; for he hath greatly withstood our words.
16At my first answer no man stood with me, but all *men* forsook me: *I pray God* that it may not be laid to their charge.
Ephesians 4:11-12 (Evaluating our motivations/ spiritual gifts)
11And he gave some, apostles; and some, prophets; and some, evangelists; and some, pastors and teachers; 12For the perfecting of the saints, for the work of the ministry, for the edifying of the body of Christ:

Colossians 4:15-17 (Empower and encourage others)

15Salute the brethren which are in Laodicea, and Nymphas, and the church which is in his house. 16And when this epistle is read among you, cause that it be read also in the church of the Laodiceans; and that ye likewise read the *epistle* from Laodicea. 17And say to Archippus, Take heed to the ministry which thou hast received in the Lord, that thou fulfill it.

Matthew 20:25-29 (Servant heart)

[25]But Jesus called them *unto him*, and said, Ye know that the princes of the Gentiles exercise dominion over them, and they that are great exercise authority upon them. [26]But it shall not be so among you: but whosoever will be great among you, let him be your minister; [27]And whosoever will be chief among you, let him be your servant: [28]Even as the Son of man came not to be ministered unto, but to minister, and to give his life a ransom for many.

Matthew 28:18-20 (Great Commission believer)

[18]And Jesus came and spake unto them, saying, All power is given unto me in heaven and in earth. [19]Go ye therefore, and teach all nations, baptizing them in the name of the Father, and of the Son, and of the Holy Ghost: [20]Teaching them to observe all things whatsoever I have commanded you: and, lo, I am with you alway, *even* unto the end of the world. Amen.

Acts 6:2-4 (Fullness of the Holy Spirit)

[2]Then the twelve called the multitude of the disciples *unto them*, and said, It is not reason that we should leave the word of God, and serve tables. [3]Wherefore, brethren, look ye out among you seven men of honest report, full of the Holy Ghost and wisdom, whom we may appoint over this business. [4]But we will give ourselves continually to prayer, and to the ministry of the word.

Romans 12:1-2 (Transformation and renewal)

[1]I beseech you therefore, brethren, by the mercies of God, that ye present your bodies a living sacrifice, holy, acceptable unto God, *which is* your reasonable service. [2]And be not conformed to this world: but be ye transformed by the renewing of your mind, that ye may prove what *is* that good, and acceptable, and perfect, will of God.

APPENDIX 8-B
LH101 SYLLABUS IN SPANISH

LH101 – Principios Bíblicos de Liderazgo
Plan de Trabajo
Marzo 12– Abril 8, 2005

Profesor del Curso: Dr. Víctor H. Cuartas
Correo Electrónico: **victcua@regent.edu**

Es para mí una gran bendición el comenzar este Programa en liderazgo Hispano compartiendo con ustedes algunos principios bíblicos de Liderazgo. Mi oración es que El Espíritu Santo de Dios le guíe y fortaleza durante el transcurso de este programa. Este plan de trabajo contiene toda la información que usted necesita conocer para llevar a cabo este curso.

Descripción del Curso
El curso proporciona la orientación general al certificado del liderazgo, su proceso y las esperanzas en la educación teológica no-formal así como orientación específica al Programa del Certificado del Liderazgo. El curso presenta principios Bíblicos importantes para el liderazgo. La atención especial es dada a Jesús como nuestra base de líder modelo y las implicaciones actuales en nuestro diario vivir.

> ➤ Se enfoca en los principios bíblicos que muestran como Jesús estuvo dispuesto a ejercer principios de liderazgo.
> ➤ Ayuda a identificar fortalezas y debilidades en la vida del estudiante, y a ver a Jesús como modelo de liderazgo.

Este curso es dictado semi-presencialmente. Durante el día **12 de marzo** los estudiantes asisten a la Universidad de Regent para recibir la clase presencial. Durante las siguientes 3 semanas hay participación e interacción a través del Internet.

PUEDEN HABER CAMBIOS EN EL PLAN DE TRABAJO SI EL PROFESOR LO CONSIDERA NECESARIO.

Duración del Curso

El curso tiene una duración de 4 semanas. Las primeras tres (3) semanas son de diálogos en el Internet (incluyendo la clase presencial en la universidad de Regent) y la última semana es de preparación y entrega del trabajo práctico.

Objetivos del Curso

> Reconocer los principios Bíblicos relacionados al liderazgo basado en el modelo de Jesús.
> Describir y enumerar las características principales de Jesús como líder
> Identificar las áreas de nuestra vida que necesitan ser transformadas por Dios.
> Contestar y analizar una auto evaluación (Analizador de Valores-Marcela Matviuk).

Metas del Curso

> Jesús como modelo de líder personal en nuestra vida
> La importancia del carácter en el liderazgo
> Prioridades en la vida del líder
> La vida devocional del líder
> Reconociendo y fortaleciendo las debilidades del líder

Tiempo de Estudio Requerido Semanalmente

El tiempo mínimo requerido para cumplir con las participaciones y lecturas requeridas es de aproximadamente 5 horas semanalmente. Se recomienda que los estudiantes mantengan una vida devocional activa durante el transcurso del programa.

Distribución de Los Grupos

Los estudiantes recibirán un correo electrónico en donde se especificará el grupo que se les ha asignado para este curso.

> Grupo A
> Grupo B
> Grupo C

Libros Requeridos para el Curso

Los libros seleccionados para este curso deben ser leídos en su totalidad por los estudiantes. Los diálogos y participaciones semanales son basados en la selección por parte del profesor.

a) Briner, Bob and Ray Pritchard. *Jesús El Líder Modelo, Tomo I.* El Paso, TX: Editorial Mundo Hispano, 2002. ISBN# 0-311-46165-4

b) Murdock, Mike. *Secretos Del Liderazgo de Jesús.* Buenos Aires, Argentina: Editorial Peniel, 2001. ISBN# 987-9038-56-8

Evaluación del Curso LH101

La asistencia y participación del estudiante durante la clase presencial en la Universidad de Regent tendrá un valor de cuatro (4) puntos. El cuestionario *"Perfil Inicial del Estudiante"* tiene un valor de dos (2) puntos y la fecha máxima de entrega es Marzo 12 del 2005.

La clase tendrá 3 Diálogos y cada diálogo demandará un mínimo de 2 participaciones por parte del estudiante. Una de las participaciones consistirá en responder la pregunta del profesor y la otra a uno de los miembros del grupo. Se recomienda participar las veces que ustedes consideren necesario. Entre mas participación, mayor será el provecho del curso.

IMPORTANTE

La calificación para cada participación que CUMPLA los requisitos exigidos por el curso, es de un (1) punto por cada participación. El trabajo práctico al final del curso tendrá un valor de dos (2) puntos. El puntaje total del curso es de catorce (14) puntos y el puntaje mínimo requerido para que el estudiante apruebe el curso es de doce (12) puntos.

Para aprobar este curso usted deberá cumplir con los siguientes requisitos:

1. ASISTIR a la clase presencial en la Universidad de Regent. Se recomienda a los estudiantes PARTICIPAR activamente durante la clase.

1. COMPLETAR TODAS LAS LECTURAS—La honestidad es una de las cualidades mas significativas de un buen líder- Por la naturaleza de este sistema a distancia en este curso, nosotros contamos con su honestidad para completar todas las lecturas y tareas.

2. COMPLETAR EL CUESTIONARIO "PERFIL INICIAL DEL ESTUDIANTE" y otros cuestionarios que el profesor añada durante el curso.

3. PARTICIPAR Y COMPLETAR LOS TRES (3) DIALOGOS QUE INCLUYEN UN MINIMO DE DOS (2) PARTICPACIONES POR DIALOGO.

4. ENTREGAR UN TRABAJO PRÁCTICO DE DOS (2) PÁGINAS AL FINAL DEL CURSO.

5. MANTENER COMUNICACIÓN CONSTANTE CON LOS COMPAÑEROS DE ORACION que usted escogió para este programa.

6. REPORTAR EL PROGRESO DEL CURSO a su pastor o mentor.

7. Revisar diariamente su cuenta de correo electrónico y de Blackboard. El profesor enviará información valiosa semanalmente.

DIALOGOS/PARTICIPACIONES ELECTRONICAS

El éxito de este curso es el dialogar electrónicamente con tus colegas y el profesor. El estudiante participará a través de Blackboard un mínimo de DOS (2) veces por semana. Es decir, que cada alumno debe de participar con sus colegas y el profesor respondiendo a los diálogos planteados para este curso. Cada diálogo debe ser apoyado y sustentado con base en las lecturas asignadas. Se recomienda escribir por lo menos unas (100-150) palabras por cada diálogo. Tiene que ser conciso y claro.

La calificación semanal de los diálogos/participaciones tomará en cuenta lo siguiente:

1. Contenido general del diálogo

2. Referencias de los libros, revistas, artículos etc.

3. Número de palabras (No más de 150 palabras)

4. Por lo menos dos (2) PARTICIPACIONES (Una al profesor y otra a una persona del grupo).

LH101
PRINCIPIOS BÍBLICOS DE LIDERAZGO

ACTIVIDAD	FECHA	PUNTAJE
Cuestionario Perfil inicial del Estudiante	Marzo 12	2 Puntos
Clase Presencial en VA Beach Clase Presencial en Gainesville	Marzo 12	4 Puntos
Diálogos en el Internet sistema Bb 1er Diálogo	Marzo 14-19	2 Puntos
2do Diálogo	Marzo 21-26	2 Puntos
3er Diálogo	Marzo 28- Abril 2	2 Puntos
Entrega del 1er Trabajo Práctico Enviar al Profesor Víctor Cuartas victcua@regent.edu o al fax 757-366-5354	Abril 4-8 Puntaje Total	2 Puntos 14 Puntos

Trabajo Práctico al final del Curso
Durante la última semana del curso el estudiante se concentrará en desarrollar un trabajo práctico de 2 páginas. (2 puntos). Hay un trabajo ADICIONAL que es voluntario para LOS QUE QUIERAN presentarlo. La fecha máxima para entregar ambos trabajos es **abril 8 a las 6 PM**.

Guía para el envió de los trabajos

El trabajo práctico al final de la clase puede ser enviado al Profesor Víctor H. Cuartas ya sea por correo electrónico a **victcua@regent.edu**. Si el estudiante decide enviarlo

electrónicamente por archivo adjunto (Word), favor de escribir en

195

la casilla de referencia o "subject" el código del curso, grupo al cual pertenece, título del trabajo y su nombre. Por ejemplo:

LH101-Grupo 1-"Encuesta en la Iglesia"-Gumerzindo Clinton

La Fecha máxima para ENTREGAR el Trabajo Práctico
> **Abril 8 a las 6 PM.** **(Horario del este/oriente)**

Instrucciones Importantes

Para poder asegurar el desempeño satisfactorio de este programa es necesario que cada participante siga las siguientes instrucciones:

1. Cada uno de los participantes debe ser capaz de asistir a las sesiones intensivas presénciales de cada uno de las materias asignadas (Durante un sábado por materia).
2. Cada participante debe tener acceso a una computadora con conexión a Internet, ya sea en su trabajo, en la iglesia, en su casa o cualquier otro lugar con la habilidad de acceder a Internet, al menos dos veces a la semana por una hora cada vez.
3. Cada participante debe adquirir los libros y materiales de lectura asignados.
4. Los participantes deben seguir estrictamente las indicaciones y asignaciones de los instructores, incluyendo lecturas, diálogos y discusiones en línea a través de Internet, trabajos de aplicación práctica, trabajos escritos o cualquier otra actividad que el instructor proponga.
5. Mantener una comunicación efectiva con el profesor ya sea vía correo electrónico o telefónicamente. El estudiante debe tomar la iniciativa en caso de tener inquietudes o preguntas acerca de cada materia/ asignación en curso.
6. Mantener comunicación constante con los 3 compañeros de oración (mínimo) que se comprometieron a orar por usted durante este programa de liderazgo.

BIBLIOGRAFÍA

a) Briner, Bob and Ray Pritchard. *Jesús El Líder Modelo, Tomo I.* El Paso, TX: Editorial Mundo Hispano, 2002. ISBN# 0-311-46165-4

b) Murdock, Mike. *Secretos Del Liderazgo de Jesús.* Buenos Aires, Argentina: Editorial Peniel, 2001. ISBN# 987-9038-56-8

c) Sánchez, Jorge Oscar. *El Líder del Siglo XXI.* Miami, FL: Editorial Unilit, 2001. ISBN 0-7899-0759-3.

d) Batista, José D. *Atrévete a Ser un Líder*. Isabela, Puerto Rico: Isabela Printing, 1998.

e) Marshall, Tom. *Entendiendo El Liderazgo*. Miami, FL: Editorial Unilit, 1998. ISBN 1-56063-567-3

f) Maxwell, John C. *Las 21 Cualidades Indispensables de un Líder.*

g) _____, John C. *Se Todo Lo Que Puedas Ser.* Buenos Aires, Argentina: Editorial Peniel 2001. ISBN 987-9038-82-7

h) _____, J. C. *Las 21 Cualidades Indispensables de un Líder; The 21 Indispensable Qualities of a Leader*. Thomas Nelson, Inc. 2000; 2003

i) Clinton, Robert. *Clinton's Biblical Leadership Comentary.* School of World Mission Fuller Theological Seminary, 1999.

j) Artículos interesantes de liderazgo que se encuentran en el Internet:

www.intouch.org
www.injoy.com
www.ministeraldevelopment.com

¿Cómo Comunicarse con el CLAL?

➢ Rodrigo Zárate: rodrzar@regent.edu

➢ Marcela Matviuk: marcmat@regent.edu

Diálogo 1
Marzo 14 al 19 del 2005
Tema: El Liderazgo de Jesús

Objetivos del Primer Diálogo

➢ Identificar las características más importantes de Jesús como modelo de líder.
➢ Las dos áreas del "Perfil Del Estudiante" que se enfatizarán en esta clase son:
  o *Reconocer y seguir el ejemplo del liderazgo de Jesús*
  o *Reconocer claramente nuestras debilidades y fortalezas*

Material de Lectura:

➢ Libro "Secretos del Liderazgo de Jesús" de Mike Murdock. Leer el capítulo 1 (Páginas 11 a 14), el capítulo 2 (Páginas 15 a 18) y el capítulo 3 (Páginas 19 a 21).

Pregunta para el primer diálogo (2 participaciones)

En los primeros tres capítulos del libro "Secretos del Liderazgo de Jesús", Mike Murdock comparte tres características de Jesús como líder.

1) ¿Cuáles son las características?

2) ¿Con cuál de las tres características usted se identifica más y por qué?

3) Comparta por lo menos un pasaje bíblico que describa la importancia de estas características en la vida de Jesús como líder.

Diálogo 2
Marzo 21 al 26 del 2005
Tema: Inventario Personal

Objetivos del segundo dialogo:

➢ Descubrir las fortalezas y las debilidades en nuestra vida, y como afectan nuestro manera de guiar y servir a otros.

Leer y meditar en Efesios 5:15-17 (RV- 1995)

[15]Mirad, pues, con diligencia cómo andéis, no como necios sino como sabios, [16]aprovechando bien el tiempo, porque los días son malos. [17]Por tanto, no seáis insensatos, sino entendidos de cuál sea la voluntad del Señor.

Material de Lectura

➢ Libro "Secretos del Liderazgo de Jesús" de Mike Murdock. Leer los capítulos 21 al 24 (Páginas 84 a 95).

Pregunta para el segundo Diálogo (2 participaciones)

➢ Con base en las lecturas de los capítulos 21 al 24:

1) ¿Qué áreas usted necesita cambiar actualmente?
2) Identifique y describa por lo menos dos (2) obstáculos que se le presentan para que usted pueda cambiar dichas áreas.
3) ¿Qué pasos considera usted tomar hoy para fortalecer dichas áreas?

Nota: Incluir pasajes bíblicos en su participación.

Diálogo 3
Marzo 28 a Abril 2 del 2005
Tema: Estableciendo Prioridades

Objetivos del tercer dialogo

➢ Comparar los principios bíblicos de liderazgo con los modelos de liderazgo de la sociedad actual.

Material de Lectura:

> Libro "Jesús, El Líder Modelo", Tomo I. de Bob Briner y Ray Pritchard. Leer los siguientes 4 capítulos: Capítulo 6 (Páginas 32 y 33), capítulo 19 (Páginas 65 y 66), capítulo 33 (Páginas 97 y 98) y el capítulo 51 (Páginas 139 y 140).

Pregunta para el tercer Diálogo (2 participaciones)

1) ¿Describa 2 características del liderazgo de Jesús que más le impactaron en su vida personal? Explique su respuesta.
2) ¿Cuál de las características de liderazgo presentadas por el autor considera usted es la que más necesita ser practicada en su comunidad, y por qué?

IMPORTANTE: Les recuerdo que la próxima semana deben terminar el Trabajo Práctico. La fecha máxima para enviar el trabajo es el 9 de abril. Las instrucciones del trabajo final están a continuación.

Trabajo Práctico (Al final del curso)
Fecha de Entrega: Abril 8 – hasta las 6 PM
Tema: Compartiendo lo Aprendido

En un documento de dos (2) páginas identificar algunos pasajes Bíblicos claves que resaltan el modelo de Jesús como líder y luego entreviste a (2) personas de su iglesia y (2) personas de la comunidad (Que no son creyentes) y formule las siguientes preguntas:

Nota: En el caso de los pastores que están tomando el curso, favor de entrevistar a (2) pastores y (2) líderes no creyentes de la comunidad.

Nombre Completo: _____

Nacionalidad:_____   Edad_____Años

¿Cuántas personas conforman su grupo familiar? _____

Marque con una "x" la respuesta correcta

Sexo: Masculino (M)___ Femenino (F)___

Estado Civil: Soltero(a) ____ Casado(a) ___ Divorciado(a) __
Viudo(a)_____

Favor de contestar las siguientes preguntas:

1) Reconoce y sigue el ejemplo del liderazgo de Jesús (Marque con una "x" la respuesta mas acertada. El 1 es el menor y el 10 es el mayor).

(**POCO**)   1   3   5   7   10   (**MUCHO**)

2) ¿Qué significa ser un líder Cristiano en la sociedad actual?
3) ¿Cuál es el propósito del liderazgo?
4) ¿Cuál es la característica más importante de un líder y por qué?
5) ¿Qué importancia tiene el carácter en la vida de un líder?
Al final de la encuesta incluya las respuestas de las (4) personas y compare las respuestas entre los 2 grupos (creyentes y no creyentes). ¿Qué similitudes y diferencias encontró? Escriba su opinión y concusión personal en el trabajo escrito.

Sugerencia: los miembros de una misma iglesia que están tomando este curso pueden compartir luego sus trabajos y experiencias. En un futuro pueden preparar una clase de liderazgo durante la escuela dominical o sección de entrenamiento de la iglesia.

Trabajo Adicional (Voluntario)
Fecha de Entrega: Abril 8 Hasta las 6 PM
Tema: El Líder y la Oración
En el siguiente pasaje de la Biblia (Compubiblia, Versión Reina Valera 1995) encontramos a Jesús resaltando principios importantes para nuestro liderazgo personal. El pasaje se encuentra en el Evangelio de Marcos Capítulo 1, versículos del 35 al 42:

[35]Levantándose muy de mañana, siendo aún muy oscuro, salió y se fue a un lugar desierto, y allí oraba. [36]Lo buscó Simón y los que con él estaban, [37]y hallándolo, le dijeron:

—Todos te buscan.
³⁸Él les dijo:
—Vamos a los lugares vecinos para que predique también allí, porque para esto he venido.
³⁹Y predicaba en las sinagogas de ellos en toda Galilea, y echaba fuera los demonios.
⁴⁰Vino a él un leproso que, de rodillas, le dijo:
—Si quieres, puedes limpiarme.
⁴¹Jesús, teniendo misericordia de él, extendió la mano, lo tocó y le dijo:
—Quiero, sé limpio.
⁴²Tan pronto terminó de hablar, la lepra desapareció del hombre, y quedó limpio.

Instrucciones

Teniendo en cuenta la lectura y meditación del pasaje bíblico asignado, responda:
1. ¿Qué principios de liderazgo encuentra en este pasaje?
2. ¿Qué pasos prácticos está usted dispuesto a tomar hoy para aplicar los principios aprendidos en este pasaje?

APPENDIX 9A
BLACKBOARD STATISTICS FOR LH101

Area ID	Hits	%
Address Book	0	0
Announcements	753	9.2
Glossary	0	0
Calendar	0	0
Chalk Title Management	0	0
Collaboration	2	0
Content Area	285	3.5
Communications Area	41	0.5
Email	145	1.8
Roster	22	0.3
Tools Area	65	1.0
Discussion Board	6	0.1
Dropbox	0	0
Homepage	1	0.
The Electric Blackboard	0	0
Groups	6702	82.1
Gradebook	19	0.2
Manual		0
Messages		0.1
Observer Tools		0
Personal Information		0.
Resources		0
Staff Information		1.0
My Grades		1.0
Tasks		0
Total	**8041**	**100**

Folder	Hits	%
Course Material	280	50.7
Syllabus	137	24.8
Assignments	123	22.3
Bibliography	8	1.4
External Links	4	1.0
Total	**552**	**100**

APPENDIX 9 B
BLACKBOARD STATISTICS FOR LH102

Area ID	Hits	%
Address Book	0	0
Announcements	753	9.2
Glossary	0	0
Calendar	0	0
Chalk Title Management	0	0
Collaboration	2	0
Content Area	285	3.5
Communications Area	41	0.5
Email	145	1.8
Roster	22	0.3
Tools Area	65	1.0
Discussion Board	6	0.1
Dropbox	0	0
Homepage	1	0.
The Electric Blackboard	0	0
Groups	6702	82.1
Gradebook	19	0.2
Manual		0
Messages		0.1
Observer Tools		0
Personal Information		0.
Resources		0
Staff Information		1.0
My Grades		1.0
Tasks		0
Total		**100**

Folder	Hits	%
Course Material	280	50.7
Syllabus	137	24.8
Assignments	123	22.3
Bibliography	8	1.5
External Links	4	0.7
Total	**552**	**100**

APPENDIX 10

SAMPLE OF INSTRUCTOR'S PROGRESS REPORT FOR LH101

Hispanic Leadership Certificate Program

Instructor Victor Cuartas

1. Course LH101

a. Description of activities

ACTIVITY	DATE	SCORE
Student Entrance Profile	March 12	2 Points
On-Campus Session	March 12	4 Points
Post-Session Dialogue in Bb 1er Dialogue	March 14-19	2 Points
2do Dialogue	March 21-26	2 Points
3er Dialogue	March 28-April 2	2 Points
Practical Project Send to Víctor Cuartas victcua@regent.edu or via fax 757-366-5354	April 4-8	2 Points
	Total Score	14 Points

b. Description of how activities were carried out:

The orientation and the first session on campus were very good. The students were so exited and most of them had good participation. The dialogues through the Blackboard system were very interested and in general I was so pleased with the participation of the students.

The students were participating through the Internet by using the Blackboard system for three consecutive weeks. They posted a minimum of two dialogues per week.

At the end of the class the students were asked to write a two-page practical paper and they worked hard to finish well.

206

c. Description of any difficulties in carrying out activities

Most of the challenges were in terms of the computer competency and use of the blackboard system. Some of them had some difficulties installing the appropriate software to get Internet connection. Because of that I encouraged them to work as a team so that everybody can finish well.

d. Justification of any major changes to the original plan (content related)

In terms of content, I did not change anything so we followed the description of the syllabus. In regards to the activities thank God everything was done according to the initial plan and dates.

2. Outcome

a. Description of the outcomes of the activities, including any reasons for not achieving desired outcomes.
I am very pleased with the outcome of the class. All the students (22) passed the class and fulfilled the minimum requirements of the course.
Even though some of them experienced some family problems, they overcame the obstacles and received the support from God and from his/ her classmates. At the end they got a sense of unity and accomplishment.
It was a blessing for me to teach this class and I also learned a lot from every group.

b. What changes have occurred in the program as a result of the outcomes?

No changes have occurred in the program so far. Everything was done as planned from the beginning.

Blessings in Christ Jesus,
Professor Victor H. Cuartas

APPENDIX 11
INTERVIEW QUESTIONS FOR HLCP

1. Personal presentation: tell us your name, what do you do, including your experience in your church.

2. How was your experience in the Hispanic leadership Certificate Program?

3. What did you learn about the leadership of Jesus and the Biblical principles that more affected you?

4. How the to learn about leadership based on the model of Jesus helps you in the personal level and to your church/community/country? CONCRETE EXAMPLES.

5. What have you changed in your person and in your conduct since finished the classes LH101 and 102?

6. What do you think that others see different in you since the culmination of the program?

7. What did you learn additionally about the use of computers and Blackboard system?

8. How has it changed your level of commitment with God and with the church now that you have finished this program?

9. How do you see now leadership in general?

10. Why would you recommend this program to others?

END NOTES

[1] U.S. Census Bureau, *The Hispanic Population in the United States: March 2002,* Current Population Reports, P20-545 (Washington D.C.: GPO), 1-2.

[2] U.S. Bureau of the Census, 2000 *Census of Population & Housing* (Washington D.C.: GPO, 2000).

[3] U.S. Census Bureau, Population Division, Table CO-EST2002-ASRO-02-51 (Washington D.C.: GPO, 2003).

[4] John M. Davis, interview by author, Virginia Beach, VA, 15 September 2005.

[5] Juanita Weiss, interview by author, Virginia Beach, VA, 18 January, 2005

[6] Leslie Harris, interview by author, Hampton, VA, 19 January, 2005

[7] U.S. Census Bureau, *The Hispanic Population in the United States*, 4.

[8] Ibid, 1.

[9] James T. Flynn, Wie L. Tjiong, and Russell W. West, *A Well-Furnished Heart: Restoring the Spirit's Place in the Leadership Classroom* (Fairfax, VA: Xulon Press, 2002), 89.

[10] Aubrey Malphurs, *Values-Driven Leadership: Discovering and Developing Your Core Values for Ministry* (Grand Rapids: Baker, 1996), 34.

[11] Ibid, 156.

[12] Flynn, Tjiong, and West, 210.

[13] Ibid, 208.

[14] Robert Banks, *Reenvisioning Theological Education: Exploring a Missional Alternative to Current Models* (Grand Rapids: Eerdmans, 1999).

[15] Leroy Ford, *A Curriculum Design Manual for Theological Education* (Nashville: Broadman, 1991).

[16] Lois B. Easton, *The Other Side of Curriculum: Lessons from Learners* (Portsmouth, NH: Heinemann, 2002).

[17] Ibid, 78, 94.

[18] E. Michael Connelly and D. Jean Clandinin, *Teachers as Curriculum Planers: Narratives of Experience* (New York: Teachers College Press, 1988).

[19] Ibid, 4.

[20] Robert W. Ferris, *Establishing Ministry Training: A Manual for Programme Developers* (Pasadena, CA: William Carey Library, 1995).

[21] Ibid, 22.

[22] Ibid, 45.

[23] J. Robert Clinton, *The Making of a Leader* (Colorado Springs, CO: Navpress, 1988).

[24] Ibid, 204.

[25] Joseph Umidi, *Confirming the Pastoral Call* (Grand Rapids: Kregel Publications, 2000).

[26] Ibid, 20.

[27] Ibid, 61.

[28] Ibid, 98.

[29] Eugene H. Peterson, *Working the Angles: The Shape of Pastoral Integrity* (Grand Rapids: Eerdmans, 1987).

[30] Marva Dawn and Eugene Peterson, *The Unnecessary Pastor: Rediscovering the Call* (Grand Rapids: Eerdmans, 2000). 63-77.

[31] Henri Nouwen, *In the Name of Jesus: Reflections on Christian Leadership* (New York: Crossroad, 1998).

[32] Ibid, 53.

[33] Roger Heuser and Norman Shawchuck, *Leading the Congregation: Caring for Yourself While Serving Others* (Nashville: Abingdon, 1993): 46-47.

[34] Eric H. F Law, *The Wolf Shall Dwell With the Lamb: A Spirituality for Leadership in a Multicultural Community* (St. Louis: Chalice, 1993): 14-16.

[35] Ibid., 91

[36] Ibid., 97.

[37] Ray Bakke, *A Theology as Big as the City* (Downers Grove: 1997).

[38] George F. Simons, Carmen Vasquez, and Philip R. Harris, *Transcultural Leadership: Empowering the Diverse Workforce* (Houston, TX: Gulf, 1993).

[39] Ibid, 82.

[40] Ibid, 34.

[41] James D. Whitehead and Evelyn Eaton Whitehead, *Method in Ministry: Theological reflection and Christian Ministry* (Kansas City, MO: Sheed & Ward, 1995).

[42] Ibid, 4-5.

[43] Ortiz, Manuel, *One New People: Models for Developing Multiethnic Church* (Downers Grove: InterVarsity, 1996).

[44] Ibid, 135-137.

[45] Justo L. González, *Mañana: Christian Theology from a Hispanic Perspective* (Nashville, Abingdon, 1990).

[46] Ibid.

[47] Samuel Solivan, *The Spirit, Pathos and Liberation* (Sheffield, England: Sheffield Academic Press, 1998).

[48] Eldin Villafañe, The Liberating Spirit Berating Spirit: Toward an Hispanic American Pentecostal Social Ethic (Grand Rapids: William B. Eerdmans, 1993).

[49] Ibid.

[50] Ibid.

[51] Eldin Villafañe, Bruce W. Jackson, Robert A. Evans, and Alice Frazer Evans, *Transforming the City: Reframing Education for Urban Ministry* (Grand Rapids: William B. Eerdmans, 2002).

[52] Ibid, 5-9.

[53] Kenneth G. Davis and Edwin I. Hernandez, *Reconstructing the Sacred Tower: Challenge and Promise of Latino: A Theological Education* (Scranton, PA: The University of Scranton Press. 2003).

[54] In 1988, Justo L. González wrote a report commissioned by The Fund of Theological Education entitled *The Theological Education of Hispanics* (Atlanta, GA).

[55] Davis and Hernandez.

[56] Ibid.

[57] Alex Montoya, *Hispanic Ministry in North America* (Grand Rapids: Zondervan, 1987).

[58] Edwin Hernandez, Kenneth Davis, and Catherine Wilson, "The Theological Education of U. S. Hispanics," *Theological Education* 38, no. 2 (2002): 71-85.

[59] Ibid, 72.

[60] Ibid, 64.

[61] Ibid, 74.

[62] Edwin Hernandez, Kenneth Davis, and Catherine Wilson, "The National Survey of Hispanic Theological Education," *Journal of Hispanic/Latino Theology* 8, no. 4 (2001): 37-59.

[63] Ibid, 37.

[64] Ibid, 58.

[65] Ibid, 56.

[66] Manuel J. Mejido, "U.S. Hispanics/ Latinos and the Field of Graduate Theological Education," *Theological Education* 34, no. 2 (1998): 59-71.

[67] Ibid, 65.

[68] Kenneth G. Davis, "The Attraction and retention of U. S. Hispanics to the Doctor of Ministry Program," *Theological Education* 33, no. 1 (1996): 75-82.

[69] Ibid., 80.

[70] Rosendo Urrabazo, "Pastoral Education of Hispanic Adults," *Missiology* 20, no. 2 (2001): 255-60.

[71] J. Robert Clinton, *The Bible and Leadership Values: A Book by Book Analysis* (Altadena, CA: Barnabas, 1993), 77.

[72] William Sanford La Sor and others, eds., *Old Testament Survey: The Message, Form, and Background of the Old Testament,* 2d ed. (Grand Rapids: Eerdmans, 1996), 142.

[73] J. Robert Clinton, *Leadership Perspectives: How to Study the Bible for Leadership Insights* (Altadena, CA: Barnabas, 1993), 104.

[74] Clinton, *The Bible and Leadership Values,* 78.

[75] Matthew Henry, *Concise Commentary on the Whole Bible* (Nashville: Thomas Nelson, 1997), 330.

[76] Donald J. Wiseman, *Tyndale Old Testament Commentaries. 1 & 2 Kings: An Introduction & Commentary* (Downers Grove: InterVarsity, 1993), 195.

[77] Ibid, 195.

[78] T. R. Hobbs, *2 Kings, Word Biblical Commentary,* vol. 13 (Waco, TX: Word Books, 1985), 20.

[79] Ibid, 20.

[80] Paul R. House, *1, 2 Kings: The New American Commentary,* vol. 8 (Nashville: Broadman & Holman, 1995), 258.

[81] Wiseman, 195.

[82] Hobbs, 21.

[83] I. W. Slotki, *Kings, Hebrew Text & English Translation with an Introduction and Commentary* (London: The Soncino Press, 1966), 72.

[84] Walter Brueggemann, *1 & 2 Kings, Smyth & Helwys Bible Commentary* (Macon, GA: Smyth & Helwys, 2000), 298.

[85] Russell H. Dilday, *1, 2 Kings, The Communicator's Commentary,* vol. 9 (Waco, TX: Word Books, 1987), 270.

[86] Wiseman, 197.

[87] Hobbs, 24.

[88] House, 265.

[89] Dilday, 294.

[90] Ibid, 300.

[91] Brueggemann, 331.

[92] Hobbs, 170.

[93] House, 308.

[94] William M. Ramsay, *The Education of Christ* (New Canaan, CT: Keats, 1981), 32.

[95] William G. Blaikie, *The Public Ministry of Christ* (Minneapolis: Klock & Klock, 1984), 22.

[96] Ibid, 25.

[97] William C. Spohn, *Go and Do Likewise* (New York: Continuum, 1999), 130.

[98] Robert E. Coleman, *The Master Plan of Evangelism* (Old Tappan:, NJ: Fleming H. Revell, 1964).

[99] A. B. Bruce, The Training of the Twelve: Timeless Principles for Leadership Development (Grand Rapids: Kregel, 1988), 52.

[100] Coleman, 73.

[101] Ibid., 75.

[102] Edwin D. Freed, *The New Testament: A Critical Introduction* 3rd. ed. (Stamford, CT: Wadsworth Thompson, 2001), 115.

[103] Blaikie, 113.

[104] Graham N. Stanton, *The Gospels and Jesus* (New York: Oxford University Press, 1989), 204.

[105] J. D. Jones, *The Apostles of Christ* (Minneapolis: Klock & Klock, 1982), 17.

[106] Coleman, 77.

[107] Ibid., 78.

[108] Bruce, 41.

[109] Coleman, 79.

[110] *BibleWorks 4: The Premier Biblical Exegesis and Research Program. Software for Windows* Version 4, (Big Fork, MT: 1999).

[111] Carl F. Henry, ed, *The Biblical Expositor: Matthew to Revelation* 2d ed, vol. 3 (Philadelphia: Holman. 1960), 80.

[112] *BibleWorks,* 4.

[113] Frederick C. Grant, Nelson's *Bible Commentary: New Testament, Matthew-Acts* vol. 6 (New York: Thomas Nelson & Sons, 1962), 152.

[114] Johnnie C. Godwin, *Layman's Bible Book Commentary: Mark* vol. 16 (Nashville: Broadman Press, 1979), 37.

[115] *BibleWorks*, 4.

[116] Ralph A. Earle, Elwood Sanner, and Charles L. Childers, *Beacon Bible Commentary*, vol. 6 (Kansas City, MO: Beacon Hill Press, 1964), 294.

[117] Clifton, J. Allen, ed. *The Broadman Bible Commentary: General Articles Matthew-Mark*, vol. 8, *Mark*, by Henry Turlington (Nashville: Broadman, 1969), 314.

[118] Henry, 84.

[119] *BibleWorks*, 4.

[120] W. K. Clarke, *Concise Commentary on the Whole Bible.* (New York: Macmillan, 1953), 699.

[121] Ibid., 699.

[122] *BibleWorks*, 4.

[123] Frank E Gaebelein, ed. *The Expositor's Bible Commentary: John-Acts,* vol. 9 (Grand Rapids: Zondervan, 1981), 136.

[124] Robert J. Karris, *The Collegeville Bible Commentary: New Testament* (Collegeville, MN: The Liturgical Press, 1992), 1003.

[125] Kenneth L Barker and John R. Kohlenberger III, *Zondervan NIV Bible Commentary: New Testament,* vol. 2 (Grand Rapids: Zondervan, 1994), 346.

[126] Henry, *The Biblical Expositor*, 179.

[127] Ralph A. Earle and Joseph H. Mayfield. *Beacon Bible Commentary* vol. 7 (Kansas City: Beacon Hill, 1965), 184.

[128] Barker, 354.

[129] Nolan B Harmon, ed. *The Interpreter's Bible: Acts-Romans* vol. 9 (Nashville: Abingdon Press, 1954), 73.

[130] J. Robert Clinton, *Clinton's Biblical Leadership Commentary* (Fuller Theological Seminary: 1999), 320.

[131] Robert L. Maddox, Jr., *Layman's Bible Book Commentary: Acts,* vol. 19 (Nashville: Broadman: 1979), 38.

[132] Clifton, J. Allen, ed. *The Broadman Bible Commentary: Acts-1 Corinthians,* vol. 10, *Acts* by T. C. Smith (Nashville: Broadman, 1970), 63.

[133] Bobby Clinton and Laura Raab, *Barnabas, Encouraging Exhorter: A Study in Mentoring.* (Altadena, CA: Barnabas, 1997), 12.

[134] Phil Alessi, *Biblical Foundations: Barnabas-Gift Oriented Ministry* (Charlottesville, VA: CRM Multiplication Team, 2002), 6.

[135] Clinton, *Clinton's Biblical Leadership Commentary*, 565.

[136] Harmon, 211.

[137] Carl A. Collins, Jr., Paul as a Leader: A Study of The Apostle's Role and Influence in the Field of Religious Education (New York: Exposition Press, 1955), 56.

[138] Ronald A. Ward, *Commentary on 1 & 2 Timothy & Titus* (Waco, TX: Word, 1974), 28.

[139] Thomas D. Lea and Hayne P. Griffin, Jr., *The New American Commentary: 1, 2 Timothy & Titus,* vol. 34 (Nashville: Broadman, 1992), 230.

[140] Donald Guthrie, *New Testament Introduction* (Downers Grove,: InterVarsity, 1990), 538.

[141] J. Vernon McGee. *Thru The Bible. I Corinthians through Revelation,* vol. 5 (Nashville: Thomas Nelson, 1983), 254.

[142] *BibleWorks,* 4.

[143] Ibid.

[144] Ibid.

[145] U.S. Bureau of the Census, 2000 Census of Population & Housing.

[146] Ibid., 2.

[147] Ibid.

[148] Ibid., 3.

[149] Roberto R. Ramirez and G. Patricia de la Cruz. *The Hispanic Population in the United States: March 2002.* U.S. Census Bureau,

Current Population Reports P20-545 (Washington DC: GPO)

[150] Ibid., 2.

[151] Ibid.

[152] Ibid., 6.

[153] Ibid., 5.

[154] U.S. Bureau of the Census, 2000 Census of Population & Housing. 3.

[155] Ibid., 6.

[156] "Activism Sets SBA Plan in Motion," [article online, 2005]; available from www.hispanicbusiness.com/ newsletter-archive/view.asp?sendoutid=635; Internet; accessed 10 June 2005.

[157] U.S. Bureau of the Census, 2000 Census of Population & Education.

[158] Ramirez and De la Cruz, 5.

[159] Ibid., 4.

[160] Ibid., 6.

[161] U.S. Bureau of the Census, 2000 Census of Population & Housing.

[162] Ibid.

[163] Ibid.

[164] Weldon Cooper Center for Public Service. "Growth in the Latino/Hispanic Population-Analysis, Table P11c, Hispanic population," [article online]; available from http://www.coopercenter.org/demographics/ANALYSIS%20&%20GRAPHICS/Hispanic%20Population/Analysis/index.php; Internet; accessed 17 June 2005.

[165] Ibid.

[166] See Appendix 1.

[167] See Appendix 4-A for details.

[168] See Appendixes 4-B and 4-C for details.

[169] See Appendix 4-F for details.

[170] See Appendix 4-G for details. The first number was mentioned most frequently by the respondents.

[171] See Appendix 4-H for details.

[172] See Appendixes 4-I and 4-J for details.

[173] See Appendix 5-A for details.

[174] See Appendix 5-B for the application form translated in Spanish.

[175] See Appendix 5-C for details.

[176] See Appendix 5-D for details.

[177] See Appendix 5-E for details.

[178] See Appendix 5-F for details.

[179] See Appendix 5-G for details.

[180] See Appendix 5-H for details.

[181] See Appendix 1.

[182] For details, see Appendix 5-I.

[183] See Appendix 5-J for details.

[184] See Appendix 5-K for details.

[185] See Appendixes 6-A and 6-B.

[186] See Appendixes 6-C, 6-D and 6-E for details.

[187] See Appendixes 7-A, and 7-B for description of LH 101 syllabus.

[188] See, Appendixes 8-A, 8-B, and 8-C for details.

[189] See Appendixes 8-D, and 8-E for details.

[190] See Appendices 8-F and 8-G for details.

[191] See Appendixes 9-A and 9-B for details.

[192] See Appendix 11 for interview questions.

How much more do we need to be prepared to share with a culture different from our own. ~~Issue~~ How prepared are we to share with those just like us - We are not only one with those like us we are also one with all people - We are called to unity -

Difficulty in realizing my lack of understanding and training to be effectiv with all people.

Most enlightening discussion
most difficult discussion

CPSIA information can be obtained at www.ICGtesting.com
Printed in the USA
BVOW080638050112

279836BV00003B/4/P